What others are saying about...

ᵀᴴᴱ NEXT LEVEL Entrepreneur

This book is most inspiring. It sheds immense light on a world full of "unknowns" for an entrepreneur... definitely gets you thinking; it opens up a world of opportunities... highly recommend!   ~ Kai

It seems people today lose their ability to dream or dream big, as life gets in the way and boring jobs are the norm. [This book] is the answer to today's youth [to] today's retired person...   ~ Jim Arnett

I always had an idea of what I wanted to do in the big picture, but it was just an idea. This book helped me to crystallize that idea into a real world plan...   ~ Spencer Reynolds

Not only will this book help you to craft a great strategy, it will help you to discover purpose in your life!   ~ A. Lee

This book was very easy and interesting to read...it helped me realize what my dream is and gave me the tools to pursue it... made me feel I can accomplish anything...   ~ Carly Spencer

This book helped me realize how I could grow individually and in my career! Great book! Highly recommend.   ~ Catalina

Provides great step-by-step processes used to execute/implement any entrepreneurial endeavor that anyone has a passion for. It shows one how to deal with disruptions, develop strategies, and think outside the box.   ~ Keith Ditta

This was a great read for anyone starting a small business... This book also translates to a job within a company as well.   ~Aaron

The exercises in this book made me think of how I could grow... It made me think strategically of how to go forward into the future.

What others are saying...

Thanks to this book I know how to make my business better.
~ Micah Shane Barge

George Black has created steps necessary for soul searching and implementing to become a successful entrepreneur.
~ Garrett Takach, competitor on
NBC's American Ninja Warrior and founder of Ninja Park

...*about* The Next Level Navigator®

The Next Level Navigator is strategy without all the BS!
~ Shaun Lee, founder of Truckin' Tomato

We had the good fortune of bumping into George at just the right time as we built Rackspace from an idea into a global company. George's ideas and passion helped us really elevate our ability to build a great company. I'm grateful for the contribution George made to us and recommend his work to anyone aspiring to build a great company.   ~ Lanham Napier, former CEO of Rackspace

For Rackspace, Intigro [George Black] *helped the leaders of a critical new business unit create its strategy for success, and helped roll out key financial metrics. After that success, George led all our corporate off-site meetings for many years using his Next Level Navigator process. From 2004-2008, George coached many members of our leadership team to keep our strategy on track while we grew more than 50% per year. George delivered great results. I recommend him and Intigro to any business.*
~ Graham Weston, former Chairman of Rackspace

George and Intigro have a process [The Next Level Navigator] *that brings order to disarray and can help any organization focus its efforts on the key drivers of success.*
~ Lew Moorman, former President of Rackspace

THE

NEXT LEVEL

ENTREPRENEUR

Focus your Passions
Map your Direction
Build a Great Company

Fourth Edition

GEORGE BLACK

Foreword by Stephen E. Takach, Ph.D.

iP
intigrō®
Press

To Brandon
May you Live
Truly Free!
Gay

For my sons Jeremy and Jason,
and those entering the arena or already there.

It is not the critic who counts, not the man who points out
how the strong man stumbled, or where the doer of deeds
could have done better.
The credit belongs to the man who is actually in the arena,
whose face is marred by dust and sweat and blood,
who strives valiantly,
who errs and comes short again and again,
who knows the great enthusiasms, the great devotions, and
spends himself in a worthy cause,
who at best knows achievement and
who at the worst if he fails at least fails while daring greatly,
so that his place shall never be with those cold and timid
souls who know neither victory nor defeat.

~ Theodore Roosevelt
From a speech given in Paris at the Sorbonne in 1910.

Tune your ears to wisdom, and concentrate on understanding.
Cry out for insight, and ask for understanding.
Search for them as you would for silver;
seek them like hidden treasures.

~ King Solomon
Regarded as the wisest man to have ever lived,
and perhaps, the wealthiest.

~ Contents ~

~ Contents ~

Foreword

Imagine what it would feel like to live fully into the person
you are meant to be.
Imagine the comfort of knowing that each step you are taking is
toward the place you are meant to go.
Imagine the conviction and trust in knowing each day what you are
doing is helping you get there.
Embedded in this vision are the answers to 3 humbling questions:
Who are you?
Where are you going?
How will you get there?
You may not have the answers now, but after reading *The Next
Level Entrepreneur* and engaging the exercises within, you will.

An old business adage states *"under promise and over deliver"*.
So why do I make such a bold claim to begin this foreword?
Because consistent with the adage, what is answered above is just
the beginning of what will be delivered.

The *freedom* that I feel every day by living into my truest self
comes from my understanding of who I am, which I now know
because of the process in this book.

The *comfort* that I feel every day through knowing that the
actions I take are leading me to where I am intended to be, was
bestowed upon me after reading this book.

The *determination* and *clarity* that I feel every day in all my
strides to reach where I am headed has never been more certain,
since my engagement with this book.

This text that is before you and the process within has enabled
me to know my purpose here on this earth, my purpose in this life,
my one song to sing; which is to help others go from who they are

today, to who they may become.

Before engaging with this book and the process within I always knew I wanted to help others. I could feel it. I just did not know how. I did not know where all my actions were leading. Now I can state with conviction that my promise to all in this world is that when they interact with me they will feel comfort through trust, and they will experience transcendence through community.

I am empowered to face each day with drive and purpose, eagerness and will, honor and the ultimate privilege of having a sense of knowing the answer to life's big question:

What in the world am I here on this planet for?

If having this kind of assurance is something that you seek, if making this kind of bold statement is something that you desire, if peace within is something that you long for, then reading this text before you is the first step.

Engaging the exercises inside the book is the second step. As a third step seek a community of which you are a contributing part to encourage you. These steps are how you can go from who you are today to who you will become at your Next Level.

Many authors pour themselves into their writing to create a text that is good, however few authors offer good news that is worth spreading. I agreed to write this foreword because the text before you is good news worth spreading.

Please believe me when I tell you that you are more than the sum of the knowledge you attain or the things that you create. Allow me to leave you with one last question:

How long do you want to continue before knowing these
answers for yourself?

Read on,

Stephen E. Takach
PhD, Strategic Management

Preface: Finding a Sage!

...*a what?*

A recent search on amazon.com revealed 2,129,044 books on business. Really!?! Honestly now, do we need a 2,129,045th book on business? Probably, not.

What we do need are significant relationships that encourage us to move in the direction of our dreams providing us with wisdom and clarity.

Today, the world of business is fast paced, highly measured, and demanding instant results. A great picture of this can be found in most airports. It is easy to spot the business people striving for success. They are moving fast, not wasting a moment, plugged into one or more electronic devices. Over time this pace can be disorienting. In fact, so disorienting that we may not even be aware that we have lost our bearings.

So, what is this success we are chasing?

Do any of us really have a clear finish line? A finish line that when crossed, we could know true success and celebrate it.

In reality, it may seem clearer to know when we have failed. Occasionally, we may even ask ourselves: "Now, why did I accept this position? Or, pursue this career? Or, start this enterprise?"

For some, the answer may be found deep within them as a buried entrepreneurial desire. President Theodore Roosevelt described it this way:

> *"To enter the arena..., to risk..., strive valiantly..., to be tested, proven..., ultimately knowing victory or defeat..., but never to be counted with the faint-hearted."*

So what if you, dear reader, met a person who had gone before you and pursued their entrepreneurial dreams? Who had entered the arena? Who has known both successes and failures? And, who was willing to speak deeply to you about it all? And even more significantly, a person who was willing to provide discernment into your life about specific moments you are facing?

Who in fact is a sage. A what?

A person of profound wisdom, *a sage*; not to be confused with the aromatic plant or sagebrush!

But, what about a business mentor or coach, a counselor, even a consultant? Are they sages? Not necessarily. Typically, they are people you trust and can bring great value. They have more experience, they advise, encourage and may even provide some training.

A sage can be all this and more, but they are different. A sage brings keen wisdom, deeper insights, and illuminating discernment to the person they are guiding. They bring interpretation to life events. They focus on what is truly important for that person.

Experiencing a sage can feel like slowing down or even going in reverse, only to discover that somehow you ended up far ahead of where you expected to be.

After encountering a sage one can have a truer understanding of their circumstances and themselves, and are often stirred to pursue the greater treasures in life.

So, how valuable would a relationship with someone of deep wisdom, significant real life experience, and true discernment be to you? Someone who helps you interpret life? Priceless, right!?!

Yet, why do most of us not have a sage in our life?

Maybe it is because our youth oriented culture does not value their contribution. Or, those who could be sages do not believe they have much to offer. Or, there simply are not many sages.

But, wait!

Preface

What if sages were meant to be hard to find?
Much like a rare gem or an expensive mineral is hard to find.
After all, how many true sages have you ever met?

Yet instead of seeking a sage, we buy 2,129,044 books on
business looking for a new concept or an inspiration or a quick fix,
so we can better navigate the world of business, and even life itself.

This book is a collection of letters beginning July 10, 1941.
A young man, Max North, has no idea where to begin with his
entrepreneurial ambitions. Hoping for some sage advice, he writes a
letter to Mr. A. This renowned entrepreneur has wealth beyond
money that includes such treasures as wisdom and understanding.

Max is astonished, grateful, and puzzled by Mr. A's response,
because Mr. A directs Max into the source of his entrepreneurial
desires, his dreams. A secret that every entrepreneur should
periodically revisit. In fact, throughout this correspondence Mr. A
will *reveal even more secrets of an entrepreneur*!

Now, we all know that life does not occur in a vacuum. There are
joys and tragedies; setbacks and victories. This is when life is most
real, and the same is true for Max.

Mr. A is available for Max in these times providing guidance,
insight, and interpretation to help him negotiate the ups and downs
of life. He shows Max how to use these life experiences to *focus his
entrepreneurial desires, chart his own course, and launch a great
company*.

Over this five year correspondence, there are gaps between some
letters. So to provide context and add perspective, short vignettes
have occasionally been inserted based on historical research or
other unpublished letters, journals or notes of these two men.

In the spirit of Mr. A's zeal for all to *focus their passions* there are
special pages titled:

Sage Advice to Apply.

They are included in Parts 1 and 2 with the intent of aiding you in better utilizing Mr. A's counsel to Max. These applications summarize the preceding letters into questions, making it easy to turn Mr. A's advice into your own personal insights and actions.

In Part 3 Mr. A leads Max in ways to sprout his desires into a real business using his most essential secret:

The Next Level Navigator.

Map your direction by following along with Max and giving your own responses to Mr. A's guidance to develop The Next Level Navigator for your on-going company or startup. It even works for your own personal Next Level, too.

This strategic process has proven to be an invaluable tool in *building a great company*!

In conclusion, my crazy aspiration for you, dear reader, would be to do more than just read this book!

I hope you will engage the letters and processes to receive sage advice that you can apply to everyday life, experience new freedoms by living more fully into the person you are intended to be, and achieve many breakthroughs towards all your future Next Levels.

Therefore, my best suggestion in reading this book is:

First, read the entire book all the way through and enjoy the entrepreneurial journey of Max with Mr. A.

Second, return to the Sage Advice summaries and do those.

Third, complete The Next Level Navigator for your business or startup, a group you may lead, or even for yourself. (For more resources see page 217 or go to LiveTrulyFree.com.)

Oh, and one more thing:

I hope that one day you meet your very own Mr. A*!*

~ George Black

THE

NEXT LEVEL

ENTREPRENEUR

Focus your Passions
Map your Direction
Build a Great Company

PROLOGUE: Before the Correspondence Began

The correspondence contained in these pages actually began on a lark, because Max North had a reputation for taking a dare.

Max had recently graduated from college and was employed at the grain company in Salina, Kansas. And after only a few months he began wondering if there could be more to life than working for someone else's company. For he had ideas: big ideas, entrepreneurial ideas! But he had no one to turn to for guidance.

Some accounts of the story say that Max was being teased about his business venture ideas by several co-workers. One of them challenged Max that if his ideas were so good, why not ask the opinion of the famous entrepreneur, C. Marco Aureliano, who was now a well established, business magnate in New York City. No one actually believed Max would take the dare. He did, but not like they expected.

Instead, the young and bold Max North wrote Mr. Aureliano seeking entrepreneurial advice, not his opinion. Deep down this 21 year old hoped that he would find an entrepreneurial sage.

Somehow, Max's letter survived the layers of Mr. Aureliano's vast organization and reached his hands. The response Max received from that first letter opened the door to a fascinating correspondence and relationship that eventually covered the gamut *from the secrets of an entrepreneur to the wisdom one could apply to everyday life.*

There was an almost immediate informality to their correspondence, since Max would begin addressing Mr. Aureliano as Mr. A. Over the years a fondness would develop between these two men, similar to a father-son relationship.

These letters were copied from originals of Mr. A's and carbon copies of Mr. North's. How they were found is another story for another time. Suffice it to say, that after Mr. Max North passed away, a hidden cache of letters was unexpectedly discovered among his belongings.

As evidenced by the dates of the letters these men were living in an earlier era. However, it is extraordinary how their correspondence is as relevant today, as it was then.

~ a brief background on Max and Mr. A ~

Although many may know of the philanthropist and multi-millionaire Mr. Max North, few may know his story and even fewer may know of his relationship with the legendary entrepreneur, C. Marco Aureliano.

Born and raised on a farm in the Midwest, Max North began work at the Grain Processing Company of Salina, Kansas after majoring in Agriculture at Kansas State College of Agriculture and Applied Science. Following his entrepreneurial itch and guided by Mr. A's advice, he started a grain transportation company after World War II. It would grow into the juggernaut known as The Global Food Distribution Company.

Throughout his life, Mr. North would dedicate more and more of his resources and time to feeding, clothing, and providing medical help to the hungriest in the world. By the time of his death Mr. North had completed the transfer of all of his assets to his foundation whose sole beneficiary is the international, non-profit corporation he established: *For the Hungriest.*

Regarding Mr. Aureliano, he significantly influenced and shaped the communications industry throughout his lifetime. His numerous entrepreneurial endeavors led him to establish Sapientis International Communications through which he impacted both the communications industry and the budding technology industry of his day.

As a young man, Mr. A experienced a transfer of information that was not available to most people of that era through the telegraph. As he applied this information to his life and various business endeavors, he soon found himself growing in both knowledge and wisdom.

Mr. A recognized that knowledge or simply more information does not necessarily lead to wisdom, yet there can be a connection. However, as he began to realize the life producing benefits of wisdom and understanding, Mr. A endeavored to originate similar experiences for others.

Having studied history, especially the Founding Fathers of the United States of America, he knew that freedom, not oppression, brought about the open exchange of ideas and information. In fact, framed and hanging on the wall beside the door to his office was the final sentence from the Declaration of Independence. So, whether entering or leaving he was reminded of the source and cost of that freedom as the *ultimate adventure*:

> *" And for the support of this Declaration, with a firm reliance on the protection of Divine Providence, we mutually pledge to each other our Lives, our Fortunes, and our sacred Honor."*

Mr. A equated entrepreneurship with freedom, i.e. free enterprise. Entrepreneurs in Mr. A's view are a creative force who undertake some kind of endeavor while accepting risk with no guarantee of reward. They are a type of personality who flourish in a free society.

In his view the United States of America was the tangible result of a unique combination of knowledge, wisdom and understanding applied by the Founding Fathers that sourced in their faith and study of governments, cultures, and philosophers. Mr. A believed they were driven by their passion, as revealed in the preamble of the constitution: *"in order to form a more perfect union"*.

He recognized entrepreneurship as one of the paths to preserving freedom, and even discovering wisdom. Entrepreneurs do this without thinking, because of who they are. They see needs, opportunities and possibilities, where others do not. They respond, create, take risks, build businesses, and expand commerce to make life better.

So, Mr. A devoted himself and his company to expanding the marketplace of ideas through the encouragement of much entrepreneurial activity. In so doing, Mr. A believed he was joining with the Founding Fathers in helping to extend freedom to all people throughout the world.

But Mr. A had even deeper aspirations! Over the years he had come to understand that the greatest freedom one could ever embrace was living fully into the person they were intended to be. His hope was that every human being on earth would come to fully live into their truest self.

For you see, Mr. A had concluded that this could be done anywhere in the world regardless of circumstance. Whether one lived in the bleakest place on earth or the most glorious or anywhere in between, it was possible to experience this greatest freedom every day.

And if you really ponder Mr. A's aspiration, you may begin to realize an almost unimaginable freedom for yourself!

PART ONE: Pre-War Dreams

~ a simple letter leads to an unexpected relationship ~

*"Any one with a vision for anything is an entrepreneur.
However, life becomes a real adventure for those who
act on their vision and seize opportunity. They are the
ones who become entrepreneurs living into their dreams,
and not someone else's!"*

~ Mr. A

Max North's life illustrates that philosophy in these letters. He
seeks an answer to a seemingly simple question. That answer
produces in him more questions and draws him in deeper.

Soon he finds himself on an adventure: a quest for knowledge,
understanding and wisdom. A journey he never knew existed.

Life rarely works according to our plans. So how should one live?
plan? dream? It can all begin with one simple inquiry *to start
focusing your passions.*

Knowing the Future

Thursday, July 10, 1941

Dear Mr. Aureliano:

My name is Max North. I have been contemplating writing you for some time. Even though you don't know me, I feel as if I know you after reading many accounts of your entrepreneurial successes and failures. You are quite the inspiration to me!

Last week, I was finally spurred to send this letter after I heard President Franklin Roosevelt say in his Fourth of July speech:

> *"We know that we cannot save freedom in our own midst, in our own land, if all around us our neighbor nations have lost their freedom... And so, it is that when we repeat the great pledge to our country and to our flag, it must be our deep conviction that we pledge as well: our work, our will and, if it be necessary, our very lives."*

Mr. Aureliano, I am intrigued about free enterprise and the freedom it promotes through entrepreneurism which I know you champion. I have read about your humble beginnings in the Midwest of the United States in the late 19th century. However, what has most captivated me about your story is your rise from a simple telegraph operator for the railroads to founding the company Sapientis International Communications, now a leading force in the telecommunications industry.

Throughout your life you have navigated so many challenges like the Panic of 1893 and its aftermath, the Great War, and the Great Depression. Yet, after each obstacle you somehow rose to even greater heights. What an adventurous life you seem to have lived!

For these reasons and the fact you are a fellow Kansan, I am persuaded to correspond with you. I have grown up in the Midwest on a farm near Salina, Kansas. After graduating from college with major studies in Agriculture and special studies in the food industry, I secured a job at the Grain Processing Company in Salina.

Not to diminish my accomplishments, my problem is that I would prefer to chart my own course, rather than work as a part of another person's vision. Even though this change could mean more risk and less predictability. For you see, I have some ideas on how to transform this industry, or at least I think these ideas might transform it.

Mr. Aureliano, I am thinking I might like to become an entrepreneur, but do not know where to begin, hence my letter to you. Don't worry, I am not looking for capitalization or contacts or anything like that. Since I imagine you must be very busy, I would greatly appreciate you taking a moment to answer one question:

How did you know the future?

My hope is that your answer may help me better understand the secrets behind your success and provide some guidance.

From your story what has engaged my imagination is your vision. There are so many matters about which I would like to know, for instance: How did you determine that the telegraph would begin to cause a global revolution in the communication of mankind? How did you know that by building a business around communications it would grow into the huge company it is today?

I know your time is precious, so that is why I boiled it all down to one question.

Even as I write this, I realize that you may not be willing to share any information that could compromise your business. So, please know that even a few hints or ideas would be greatly appreciated. I thank you in advance for answering.

Best regards,
Max North
Salina, Kansas

Dreams

Monday, August 11, 1941

Dear Mr. North:

I was intrigued by your letter of July 10th, and so I desired to reply personally causing a delay in my response for which I apologize.

Many people are curious about my success, asking questions like: "how did I achieve it?" However, your enigmatic question: *"How did you know the future?"* is rare. Your question has caused me to pause and reflect, for it goes far beyond the transience of success to the depths of authenticity. By that I mean your question has taken me back many, many years. And, I thank you for that.

At the outset I must confess that I am not the great visionary you suggest, rather I was armed only with a hunch and my desires that became the seeds of a dream. Permit me to explain.

Your question implies that perhaps I was standing high on some mountain overlooking the vast future potential of communications, and I charted my course, accordingly. Actually, it felt more like I was deep in a valley surrounded by tall trees and could only see a few feet ahead, guided only by my passion and desires.

It all began as a 16-year-old sitting alone in a small telegraph office at the railway station in the little town of Tescott, Kansas, not far from Salina. Little clicks would come over the telegraph machine, I would transcribe them into messages and new worlds began opening up to me. It was exhilarating.

At that time not only did we transmit and receive messages for Western Union, but we also received news stories from New York and Los Angeles and Chicago and other major cities. I knew of events, issues, and ideas that were happening thousands of miles away before anyone else.

Through this instantaneous transfer of information, which is how it felt back in 1897, I experienced how one's knowledge could quickly increase. In short, all this learning distilled into a variety of ideas leading me into new experiences, some entrepreneurial.

In fact, I now perceive that I was growing in greater understanding and the beginning of wisdom, seemingly guided by some unseen hand. Unexpectedly, I found myself growing in various areas of my life: faith, relationships, health, business, etc.

My simple answer to your question Mr. North is that I did not know the future, instead *I dreamed the future*. Looking back, it appears I was divinely inspired to dream of a day of greater communication interactivity. Ergo, the company you see today, Sapientis International Communications, all began as a dream.

Since my days in Tescott there have been more changes in communications than in all of human history. Yet even with all these advances, my dreams have grown larger, not smaller, unlike many of my contemporaries. Today, I can imagine that communications and technology will merge, changing so much that in the next 44 years 1941 may appear old fashioned.

So, Mr. North, proper dreaming requires one to pause, reflect, and take stock of where one is in life. Unfortunately, I find that today most people are too busy to dream, for it looks as though their lives keep moving faster and faster. But if they did stop and dream, they would discover deep wells of inspiration and creativity within. And, I believe they would know a greater satisfaction in life.

I hope I have been of some help to you. I very much appreciate your writing me, and I am most happy to share with you any 'secrets' that I might have to offer. Feel free to write me anytime.

Yours truly,

Marc Aureliano
New York City

"That's It?"

Thursday, August 21, 1941

Dear Mr. Aureliano:

I was stunned to receive your letter this week! Thank you so much for personally responding to me and your kind words. Furthermore, I deeply appreciate knowing your personal thoughts behind your story and success.

After reading and rereading your letter, I simply must tell you that I remain confounded by your answer to my question: *"dreams"*?

I do not mean to sound impertinent, but the only way I can express my incredulity is: "That's it?" That's how you knew the future? That is how you began as an entrepreneur? Frankly, I was expecting something more elaborate, more complicated, well..., more sophisticated. (I hope that does not offend you; but I need to be honest about my reaction.) I mean anyone can dream, can't they?

As a result of your answer, I am bursting with more questions. So, I hope you will indulge me in one more letter and not write me off as some kind of knucklehead who will never succeed.

In your letter, you made dreaming sound so simple. I find your dreams to be gigantic, especially for a 16 year old man in a telegraph office in the middle of Kansas. I have been to Tescott, and it is tiny. So, how did you dream so big?

Unlike you, my dreams are small, if you can even call them dreams. So then my question is: How does a person dream big? Or, to put it another way, what holds someone back from dreaming such big dreams?

For example, if I described my dreams in terms of geography, my dreams might extend to the border of Saline County, Kansas. By comparison, your dreams seemed to extend beyond the Milky

Way, and you achieved them!

I am 21 years old with the world before me, as they say. I work in the office of a large grain processing operation in Salina, Kansas. My job encompasses both the operations of the plant as well as some financial aspects. My title, well I don't really have a title, but if I did it would probably be: assistant to the assistant of the assistant manager of the plant.

My dream? To become the manager of the entire plant someday when I am older. But, that is not really a dream, is it? Probably, it is more like a goal, right?

I do want to dream big, but whenever I start, I seem to always hear: "there is no way I could ever do that...", "I am not qualified...", "...not smart enough.", "...that will never work.", "what if I fail?", etc.

Aren't some dreams simply ridiculous? How does one distinguish between wishful thinking and dreams that are real and big and actionable?

I suppose what I really want to know is: *How does one dream big dreams that are truly transformative and achievable?*

Do you have any suggestions? Knowing how busy you must be, I do appreciate any insights you could give me.

Best regards,

Max North
Salina, Kansas

Infinite or Finite

Thursday, September 4, 1941

Dear Mr. North:

Let me begin by encouraging you that you are no knucklehead. I love your forthrightness and expressiveness. Your reactions are transparent and questions insightful. Your letter left me chuckling and reveals a man of no guile.

The questions you ask brilliantly cut through to the heart of the matter causing me to pause and reflect on my life, again! In fact, you show signs of having a knack for asking excellent questions, Mr. North. I have learned that it is with a curiosity similar to yours a person can seek and begin to find wisdom.

Based on your first letter, I had assumed you to be a businessman with some years of experience seeking to pursue an entrepreneurial endeavor, not a 21-year-old working as an assistant of the assistant to the assistant manager. However, I surmise that you could be a man beyond his years in maturity. This is even illustrated by your own self-observation that your dream of being the plant manager is more a goal than a dream. I tell you Mr. North, it could be both.

Any one with a vision for anything is an entrepreneur.
However, life becomes a real adventure for those who act
on their vision and seize opportunity. They are the ones
who become entrepreneurs living into their dreams, and not
someone else's!

I would hasten to add that these visions and dreams can go far beyond the limited realm of the business world.

So yes, that is it: *dreams!* But, I have discovered over the years that whereas dreaming may seem simple, it is curiously complicated. Especially when you consider that *dreams can lead to visions.*

To dream big depends on the size of your worldview and self-awareness. Do you see your world as getting larger? Or smaller? Do you see yourself as someone who can impact your world? Or who the world will impact?

Allow me to characterize it as follows. In talking with some friends of mine, who are top level astronomers and physicists, there is a current theory that states the universe is constantly expanding. What that essentially means is the universe is infinite with ever expanding possibilities.

If that is true for the universe, why could it not be true for one's worldview? Specifically, Mr. North, what about your world, the one in which you live, Saline County? Do you see it as infinite with ever expanding possibilities or as finite with limited resources?

Mr. North you observed that my dreams are considerably bigger than yours. But, I would ask you to consider if the opportunities that lay ahead for you are larger or smaller than mine. Whose world do you think is actually larger, yours or mine? Or to state it conversely, whose world has more limitations?

Before I respond further to your other questions, I would ask you to reflect on my questions in this letter. If you are so inclined, write me back your thoughts. I look forward to a continuing correspondence with you.

Sincerely yours,

Marc

New York City

P.S. Incidentally, Mr. North, please address me as Marc. I believe a less formal relationship will engender a more in-depth correspondence and friendship.

Slices of Pie

Monday, September 15, 1941

Dear Mr. A:

Thank you so much for extending your friendship to me, but I am a bit uncomfortable addressing you by your first name. Would 'Mr. A" be acceptable? And, please, just call me Max.

Since I received your letter last week, I haven't stopped thinking about it. I carry it everywhere I go. When I have a chance, I pull it out and re-read it, especially these two questions:

"Whose world do you think is actually larger: yours or mine? Or to state it conversely: whose world has more limitations?"

In your world I imagine that you have abundant resources: capital, people, assets, powerful connections... etc. which makes your world appear huge to me. That is why I compared the size of your dreams to the Milky Way.

Yet, the more I think about it, I can see how these positives could actually be limiting. I can picture how your enterprise could place large demands on you focusing you more on the present than the future. Or, the expectations of others could limit your vision. Or, after all your achievements you could become complacent and dream less, not to mention family commitments and the general demands of life. After all, it does appear to me that you have accomplished all you set out to do and that you have 'arrived'.

On the flip side, I have no wealth, no people working for me, no significant contacts, no assets, no reputation, no commitments, etc. So, nothing really holds my dreams back, except perhaps my own self-doubts or the belief that I have no way to make my dreams come true. So, are you suggesting that I am choosing to keep my dreams small?

Mr. A, you asked about my worldview and if it was expanding. I have never been out of the Midwest. Yet, as a student of history, geography, and literature, I have gone many places in many eras. Even though I have increased in knowledge I would say that my worldview remains small, like my dreams.

Until I started corresponding with you, I viewed my life like a piece of paper that is mostly blank. A blank page could seem endless with lots of room. Or it could be intimidating, wondering where do I start? Your piece of paper, i.e. your life, appears to be mostly filled, leaving less room for new ideas or dreams. Yet Mr. A, even after all your accomplishments, all your successes, all your impact; you continue to dream very big dreams.

Needless to say, your life has wrecked my metaphor because you seem to continuously operate from a mostly blank page. I find you a most remarkable man, Mr. A! How do you do it?

After all, the world about which I can dream should be much larger than the world about which you dream, but it is not. Clearly, I am missing something. Could it be that the externals of one's life may not matter nearly as much as the internals of one's life? Are there internal things in one's life that impact one's dreams?

All this reminds me of my grandmother when she would serve me one of her delicious apple or pecan pies. She would ask, "Max, is your world like this pie with only eight slices? Is it getting smaller as you eat each slice? (I usually ate 2 or 3 slices!) Or, is your world limitless, like a pie with endless slices, no matter how much is served there is always more?".

I never really understood what she meant. But now, I may be getting a clue. Just like in your letter, my grandmother was basically asking me if I saw my world as finite with limited resources or as infinite with ever expanding possibilities.

Well, I choose infinite! But Mr. A, what limits dreams? And this ties to my other questions from my previous letter:

"Are there dreams that are ridiculous? How does one distinguish between wishful thinking and dreams that are real and big and actionable?"

"...how does one have big dreams that are truly transformative and achievable?"

Can you offer me any insights?

Warmest regards,

Max North

Salina, Kansas

True Desires

Monday, September 29, 1941

Dear Max:

The moniker: 'Mr. A' will do just fine, and I shall address you as 'Max', per your suggestion.

It thrills me to know you have engaged the questions of my last letter. Your response, i.e. the questions you ask, reflect considerable thought. Inquiries of this sort can deepen understanding, and often lead to wisdom.

The answer to your questions about dreams is both simple and complicated. In a word, the simple answer is desire. Simple, because it is one word. Complicated, because *I refer to the deepest desires of the truest you.* These are hard to know, and few may understand, but I assure you they are worth pursuing.

Max, in your first letter you said that you hoped to become an entrepreneur. I find it curious you have not mentioned it again.

Some might speculate that this is a deep desire of yours, because it has led you to pursue this correspondence. Others might suggest it is not very important to you since you have only spoken of it once. I have learned it could be neither, because this entrepreneurial hope is probably a clue to even deeper desires within you.

What matters most is that you have revealed your desire to be an entrepreneur. So ask yourself: "What is that entrepreneurial desire all about?" Follow that question, and see where it leads.

One way to our deepest desires is through our dreams. Not the ones we may have while sleeping, but the dreams from our youth. Those desires and longings we had as a young person about our future.

Typically, a child dreams of what he or she can become with them as the full beneficiary of said achievement. For example, we may have dreamed of greatness as a big-league ballplayer, or elegance as a ballerina in the New York City Ballet. Or, we may have dreamed of freedom as a rancher in Texas or wealth as a tycoon on Wall Street. Or, we may have dreamed of becoming the hero as a brave law enforcement officer or person in the military. Or, we may have dreamed of great power by becoming President of the United States.

So, Max consider this question: As a youth, what were some of your dreams?

I suggest you set this letter aside and do the following: begin with a blank piece of paper and make a quick list of any dreams you remember as a youth. Do not ponder too long or analyze your memories, merely write whatever comes to mind, quickly. Then, continue reading this letter.

As we mature, our dreams hopefully deepen rather than diminish. One way they can deepen is that they become more outward focused than inward focused. In other words, our dreams become less about reaping personal benefits and more about benefitting others, that is serving the greater good of mankind. For example, we may still dream of becoming President, but our motives have changed. Instead of power and influence for oneself, the motive is serving to improve our country.

So, Max, on a separate piece of paper make a list of your dreams of today. Again, quickly list whatever comes to mind. Once you have these two lists, continue reading this letter.

With your lists in hand apply the 'dream scale' that I have rather crudely drawn below to rank your dreams. The scale is 1 to 10. A '10' is a dream that really stirs you and that you would want to pursue, and a '1' is a dream that is not as important to you, even if you achieved it.

This scale is NOT an evaluation of the dream as to its relevance,

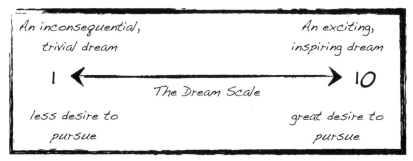

its practicality, or the chances of it ever being accomplished.

Apply the scale quickly, assigning a number to each of the dreams of your youth and your dreams of today. Follow your instincts. Allow the dream to tell you the number.

As an average, are the dreams of your youth a higher number or lower number than your dreams of today? Once you write me your results, I will share more.

Sincerely yours,

Mr. A

New York City

P.S. Max, I have just been informed that a particular business venture will bring me to Kansas City, Missouri. Would you care to join me for dinner the evening of Wednesday, November 12th?

I realize this dinner may require considerable travel time and expense for you, and would completely understand if you decline. However, I would very much enjoy meeting you in person some day, even if it is not on the 12th.

If you can come, please meet me in the lobby of the Hotel Phillips, 106 W 12th Street at 6:30 pm. I look forward to your reply.

~ Sage Advice to Apply: The Dream Scale ~

To discover where to begin as an entrepreneur, Mr. A advises Max:

"What matters most is that you have revealed your desire to be an entrepreneur. So, ask yourself: "What is that entrepreneurial desire all about?". Follow that question, and see where it leads."

Then he reveals:

"One way to our deepest desires is through our dreams."

So, Mr. A guides Max in The Dream Scale as a way for him to begin to discover his deepest desires which may provide clues as to what future entrepreneurial endeavor he might pursue.

So, how about trying The Dream Scale for yourself?

▸ Find yourself a quiet, comfortable, uninterruptible moment.

▸ Take a blank sheet of paper and write down all the dreams you can remember when you were a youth.

Hint: Remembering various moments of childhood may help you remember some of your dreams. If you ever built a treehouse, maybe you dreamed of adventure like Robinson Crusoe. Or maybe, you had a lemonade stand and dreamed of having your own business. Or maybe, you spent countless hours with LEGO® Star Wars dreaming of traveling in outer space. The dreams tied to your memories as a youth could be endless!

▸ As Mr. A advised, do NOT over-think or analyze your dreams; instead quickly write down whatever comes to mind.

▸ If you are having trouble, limit your time to less than 30 minutes for 2 or 3 sessions. Your mind will keep working on this question in between sessions.

▸ Wait a day, then grab another blank sheet of paper and write down the dreams you currently have today. Here again, write down what comes to mind. Do not analyze or think too hard.

▸ Let these lists sit for a day or two. Then apply the dream scale quickly giving each dream a number. Go with your instincts. Feel free to add any other dreams that may come to mind.

Remember Mr. A's explanation of the dream scale:

"The scale is 1 to 10. A 10 is a dream that really stirs you and that you would want to pursue, and a 1 is a dream that is not as important to you, even if you achieved it. This scale is NOT an evaluation of the dream as to its relevance, its practicality, or the chances of it ever being accomplished by you."

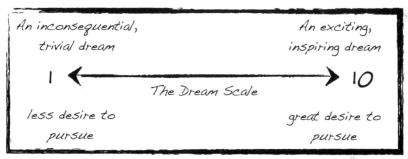

Hint: Keep referring to the dream scale as you number your dreams.

▸ Now calculate the average for your childhood dreams: total the numbers you assigned each childhood dream and divide by the number of dreams. Do the same for your current dreams.

▸ Which average is higher? Have your dreams gotten smaller or larger since childhood?

▸ Take a moment to jot down any observations about your dreams while as a youth or present day dreams. What entrepreneurial inclinations do you observe?

True Results

Tuesday, October 14, 1941

Dear Mr. A:

I am honored by your invitation to dinner, and my answer is "Yes!". I would love to meet with you in person. Thank you so much for inviting me. I will plan on meeting you in the lobby of The Hotel Philips at 6:30 pm on November 12th.

I have followed your advice and begun listing the dreams of my youth and dreams of today. I had to keep reminding myself to do it quickly and resist the urge to take my time to reflect and think over what may have been dreams then, and what are dreams today.

Soon, I was writing so fast that I am not sure from where inside me these dreams were coming. I probably wrote down dreams that I would not have remembered if I had taken more time. Something about writing on impulse was surprisingly freeing. And as I read it over, the list seems very true.

However, assigning a number to each dream was harder. Your instructions were helpful and kept me from analyzing whether I would or could actually achieve them.

For example, one of my dreams as a youth was to explore the world. I have no idea if I will ever do that, and in fact the world I dreamed of exploring back then, is different than the world I see today. There is more risk, more expense, more hardship, on and on the list goes. But in the spirit of your process, I pushed all that aside and gave that dream a '10', since it really is a dream that inspires me and I want to do it.

One of my dreams of today, is to own a home on my own piece of land. I was surprised when I only gave it a '6', but that seems correct. Interestingly, my desire to be the eventual plant manager barely made my dream list, so I gave it a '1'. I have less desire to do that dream than others.

In the end I think your process really helped me tap into something deeper and truer about me. I was a bit surprised by the results, as the dreams of my youth on the average (8.1) are considerably higher than my dreams of today (4.7).

So, now I am very curious what all this may mean. Please, do not delay your response, Mr. A!

Sincerely yours,

Max

Salina, Kansas

Disappointments

Monday, October 27, 1941

Dear Max:

I am delighted that you will be able to join me for dinner in Kansas City. Although we will have ample time to explore the topic of dreams in more detail when we meet, allow me to share some additional thoughts for your consideration.

Your 'dream scale' results are not unusual, and they may provide clues to answering a question you asked in a previous letter: "How does one have big dreams that are truly transformative and achievable?"

Over the years many people with whom I have spoken tell me that the size of their dreams diminish as they have gotten older. The reasons for this trend are as varied as the people, but a large number of these reasons can be distilled down to one common factor: disappointments. In other words, life has not met their expectations.

Consider Max, that most children rarely see limits, instead they see possibilities. Typically, they have very vivid imaginations. For example, when a boy starts to dig a hole in the back yard, he may envision himself as some great discoverer: digging through to the other side of the world reaching China. Ah, the adventure of it all!

But, let's say that he tires of the digging. Yet, this reality does not deter him or his imagination for now he has a splendid foxhole, perhaps it is the beginnings of a great fort that must be constantly manned against an ever vigilant enemy.

The dreams of youth are constantly budding and blossoming into new dreams, until...

...until some 'wise' adult comes along and informs him that he will never reach China or that his fort is just a shallow hole that needs to be refilled before someone is hurt. Some call this reality, and yes, even reality itself can be a disappointment. But truly it is this kind of disappointment, discouragement or something worse that steals imagination and kills dreams, even to the point of destroying true hope.

Yet, what could be the deeper disappointment? Simply that the 'wise' adult curtails the boy in his adventure? Or the withholding of encouragement and validation? Or worse, the withholding of themselves from joining the boy in the glory and joy of his adventure. Max, there are levels of disappointments that can lead to both indirect and direct hurts.

So what is the fate of this young boy? It all depends on how he interprets the experience. He could refute the 'wise' adult and continue to see his backyard as a gateway to new worlds of adventure, or he may allow himself to be relegated to a small patch of dirt that leads to nowhere and he becomes bored with a life that has little meaning.

One of the most intelligent men of whom I have had the honor of meeting is Albert Einstein. He is attributed with saying: "Reality is merely an illusion, albeit a very persistent one."

What a wonderful perspective, Albert, on so many levels! After all, one man's reality may not be another man's world. For you see Max, *the world around us is not always as it appears!*

Now, I ask you to reconsider the dream scale:

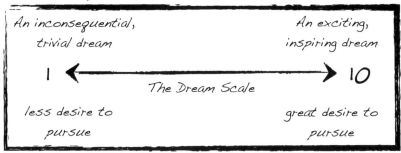

25

Using the subjective size of dreams as an indicator, an average lower than 6 or 7 could indicate that disappointments are stealing dreams. Your average suggests that the reasons your dreams do not extend beyond Saline County may be sourced in disappointments.

Max, over our lifetime we will experience all kinds of disappointments. Some may be small and quickly forgotten and others may be significant and deep like abandonment, abuse, divorce, death of a loved one, etc.

We live in a world that is broken, full of heartaches and wars and all kinds of evil. I have personally witnessed and lived through an economic panic, the Great War, and the Great Depression. Each of us have choices as to how we respond to the inevitable disappointments of this brokenness: we could embrace them, deny them, pretend they did not happen, or anesthetize the pain of them through some kind of escape. Our choice reflects how well we know who we are, our truest self, the person we are intended to be.

Regardless, all these experiences shape us deeply for good or for ill. Your grandmother's question is brilliant: "Is your pie getting smaller or are there limitless slices?". Your confusion over her question corroborates your dream scale results that even as a youth, your pie was diminishing, not limitless.

So, Max, what are some disappointments you have experienced, particularly as a youth? Gently consider this question. Take your time. Allow memories to bubble up, and when they do, jot them down. The most painful ones can be the hardest to recall. If you would like to explore this further, we can talk through any of your disappointments over dinner.

I am looking forward to our meeting with great anticipation.

Sincerely yours,

Mr. A

New York City

"...castles in the air"

Tuesday, October 28, 1941

Dear Max:

After mailing my letter of yesterday to you, I realized I wrote about disappointments based on my unstated assumption: *"castles in the air"*. This is the answer to a question of which you have been hinting: "How does an old man like me, still dream?"

According to the ancient writings of a prophet named Joel, God intends old men to dream!

> *"...I will pour out my Spirit upon all people. Your sons and daughters will prophesy. Your old men will dream dreams, and your young men will see visions."*

Yet as I have noted, many have ceased dreaming a long time ago due to unhealed disappointments. So my friend allow me to inspire your dreaming and thwart your disappointments with a vision.

Many years ago, sitting in the telegraph office I read the book: *Walden* written by Henry D. Thoreau when he was only 37 years old. I was deeply inspired by the passage he wrote on dreams and have carried it with me ever since. *(enclosed)*

Thoreau describes much more succinctly than I, the dynamic of dreams and disappointments. In essence he says that:

> *Connecting with your dreams will help you begin uncovering your deepest desires that are usually found buried under disappointments.*

However, I should warn you that this is an adventurous journey fraught with dangers!

If successful, it will lead to new freedoms and a fuller life, as Thoreau describes. For he states plainly that *"success unexpected"* results for those who move confidently towards their

I learned this, at least, by my experiment: that if one advances confidently in the direction of his dreams, and endeavors to live the life which he has imagined, he will meet with a success unexpected in common hours. He will put some things behind, will pass an invisible boundary; new, universal, and more liberal laws will begin to establish themselves around and within him; or the old laws be expanded, and interpreted in his favour in a more liberal sense, and he will live with the license of a higher order of beings. In proportion as he simplifies his life, the laws of the universe will appear less complex, and solitude will not be solitude, nor poverty poverty, nor weakness weakness. If you have built castles in the air, your work need not be lost; that is where they should be. Now put the foundations under them.

dreams. But, what are *"some things... he will put behind"* him? Based on my experience: disappointments, hurts, etc., of course!

Thoreau makes overcoming disappointments sound altogether simple, like taking off one's jacket. In reality, this is not a one time event as I described in my previous letter. In fact, there is risk in connecting with your deepest desires because I have found that you must embrace your deepest disappointments, as well. And that my friend, can be painful. So, I would advise that this journey not be taken lightly or done alone.

Nonetheless, Thoreau's description of *"passing an invisible boundary"* is precisely how it feels when one shakes free of disappointments and healing for any hurts has begun. The results are new freedoms, or as he describes: *"more liberal laws will establish themselves..."*. But, the secret result of the dynamic of dreams and disappointment is that a new kind of happiness begins to *"establish itself"*, i.e. a greater contentment in life. Thoreau describes this as *"simplifies his life...solitude will not be solitude, nor poverty poverty, etc."*.

I have observed that many people tend to avoid this adventurous journey preferring to live more on the surface of life and hope for the best. So, by playing it safe they avoid risking additional pain to discover greater freedoms. Yet, they remain a prisoner to their hidden disappointments. Not only are their lives a bit dull, but there are less freedoms and contentments, as they remain captive to their hidden disappointments which continue to shape them in detrimental ways.

Know this Max, your dreams are *"build*(ing) *castles in the air!"*, and advancing towards them is *"put*(ting) *foundations under them"*.

Therefore, may you cultivate the life long habit of *"build*(ing) *castles in the air"* and *"put*(ting) *foundations under them"* And as an old man, may you continue dreaming dreams!

Yours truly,

Mr. A

New York City

~ Sage Advice to Apply: Finding Lost Dreams ~

Among these letters we found some loose pages Max had written to help organize his thoughts in advance of his dinner with Mr. A. It appears his preparation was based on Mr. A's last two letters, especially the one dated Monday, October 27, 1941.

Max began by identifying 2 or 3 of the biggest disappointments in his life by listing a number of significant disappointments he had experienced. Max wanted to know what might have happened to diminish his dreams and desires.

To the same extent, would you be willing to go a little deeper in exploring any of your disappointments? (It does not matter if your dreams of today are larger or smaller than when you were a youth.)

> ▸ What would those significant disappointments in life be for you? What have been your biggest 2 or 3 disappointments in life? Please describe them by writing them down.

Then Max, wrote about any dreams that he associated with those disappointments.

For example: If one of your big 3 was the divorce of your parents, maybe you had a subconscious dream of growing up in a happy, intact family. Or, maybe one of your big disappointments was not achieving a certain position on a sports team or other activity and that meant your dream could not be realized. What was that dream?

> ▸ So, are there any dreams associated with your biggest disappointments? If yes, please describe them.

Next, Max used a number to measure what happened to each dream. Apparently, Max had found Mr. A's Dream Scale helpful, so he deepened it. He assigned a number between 1 and 10 to each dream. At the low end of his scale a '1' was a dream never pursued or forgotten, and at the high end a '10' was a dream fully realized.

For example: If your dream was to be an astronaut, and you did become an astronaut (or you are on track to be one), that would be a '10' on Max's Dream Scale. Or, are you an aeronautical engineer maybe that would be a '4'? Or, maybe you fly fighter planes for the Air Force, you might consider that an '8', since you almost became an astronaut. Or, maybe you never enrolled in aerospace studies or pursued a career in the Air Force, so is it an unrealized or long forgotten dream which would be a '1'.

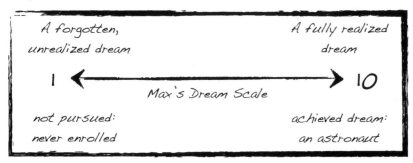

Max applied his own dream scale to his top dreams including both his youth and present day dreams plus those dreams connected to his biggest disappointments.

- Select your top (5-10) dreams from your Dream Scale as a youth, present day, and your dreams associated with the 2 or 3 biggest disappointments in your life, and list them.

- Now, assign a number between 1 and 10 per Max's scale.

- Some dreams may deserve a comment as to what happened to them (good or bad), or how you may feel about them today, or any regrets or satisfactions.

A Precipice

Monday, November 3, 1941

Dear Mr. A :

I hope this letter reaches you before you leave for Kansas City. I am very much looking forward to meeting you next week!

I was surprised to receive 2 letters from you, but they have given me much to think about. Even after several readings of both letters. I am still trying to absorb everything you wrote.

The idea of finding the truest things about me feels like I have been brought to the edge of a precipice overlooking a whole new vista that contains unlimited possibilities. However, I can only catch glimpses of these possibilities because it seems like there is a drifting fog partially blocking my complete view.

I feel both exhilarated by all the possibilities and afraid, all at the same time. Do I go forward into it, this new and unknown vista, or do I return to my old paths of familiarity? What is my hesitation? What will I find out about myself?

Could something be exposed in me that I may not really want to know? Will I find that inside me there is a harsh, aggressive man who would crush anyone in his path? Or worse, will I find a soft man who is an easy pushover? Or, will I find a man of deep conviction with the courage to act against all odds?

Mr. A, I am sure you realize that your dream scale exercise is more than just coming up with numbers for current dreams and past dreams. I now see it has been an important first step in reconnecting me with my long forgotten dreams and abandoned desires.

In the past, I dreamed of having great impact, or inventing something no one had ever heard of, or seeing the world, or dramatically doing something that makes life better for others, perhaps even influencing whole countries. However through your letters, a great part of my dreams have been exposed to include gaining power and wealth for myself.

The one question you implied, but left unasked, is now my most pressing question: *"what happened to all those dreams and desires inside me?"*.

That question has been dogging me the last few days. So, after rereading your letter of October 27th, I began to list my disappointments. One disappointment does remind me of another which triggers a memory of another. I guess this is what you meant when you said *"to let them bubble up"*.

For example, there was the disappointment of not making the baseball team in grade school or just being the backup actor in the high school play, not the lead. There was the time a teacher scolded and humiliated me in front of the class or my first girlfriend who dumped me for my best friend, a double betrayal. Then I remembered the three bullies in 6th grade who beat me up. I did not know what to do. I felt powerless and all alone, I needed my dad in that moment, but he was away on business.

The list is growing. It feels like there could be some much deeper disappointments to discover, but to be honest I'm not sure what they are. I hope to gain more insights when we meet.

I have also been thinking about your observation of my desire to be an entrepreneur. You're right, there is much more to that desire than just entrepreneurship. It ties to some of my dreams as a kid, revealed in my first letter to you: "I would prefer to chart my own course, rather than working as a part of another person's vision." When I wrote this, I did not fully realize the deep desires to which this statement is tied. With your help, I am beginning to understand.

I realize that I desire to be in an environment where I can be creative, practice leadership, set the course, affect others in a good way, shape a team of people, etc. I am not sure where all that comes from, but it seems to be more true about me than aspiring to be a plant manager, which can be a noble position for the right man, but not for me.

So, Mr. A, this leads me to a new question: *how do I find the truest things about me? After all, what on earth am I here for?*

Each day I seem to discover more clues. I am hoping our time together will be enlightening and engaging for both of us.

Safe travels,

Max

Salina, Kansas

Dining with Mr. A

Thursday, November 13, 1941

Dear Mr. A:

I will always remember last night. Never in my wildest dreams would I have thought an evening like last night could have ever happened for me. Just to meet you was an honor! And that dinner was the most incredible meal I have ever had. However, for you to spend so much time with me in sincere conversation, well… that was over the top. You are an amazing man, Mr. A! Thank you so much for taking an interest in me and for all you did last night.

To the world I know that you are regarded as a highly successful, wealthy and powerful man. Now, I am beginning to see that you possess a deeper success that the world may not understand. Even better than the meal last evening, are the breakthroughs you are helping me find in my life. Until we started corresponding I did not know such areas of my life even existed, much less that breakthrough was needed or possible.

As I rode home on the bus last night, I replayed our dinner conversation over and over in my mind. I journaled and processed as much as I could remember. (I did arrive home in time for a quick nap and was at the plant by 8 AM.)

I now realize that you are opening up a whole new world of possibilities to me. With your help I have embarked on a journey of discovery that will take some time. It was silly of me to think that all my questions could be resolved in one evening.

You have stirred me to pursue a quest of discovering what is most authentic, most true, about me. And to find answers to the question: 'what on earth am I here for?'

Right after they took away the appetizers and we were waiting on the main course you quietly sipped your drink, looked me in the eye, and asked: "Max, could you describe what your relationship with your father is similar to?".

I remember telling you some stories to give you a feel for our relationship. Then you gently pressed me with questions like "how available was he?", "what kind of input has he given me throughout my life?", "could he tell me what was truest about himself?", "did he say he was wrong when he made mistakes?" or "ask my forgiveness when he may have hurt me?", "what are my most intimate memories with my dad?".

As you kept asking these kinds of questions, I was responding with ease, almost mechanically. And then, I began to hear myself describe some of the greatest disappointments in my life. I was staggered. What happened next was totally unexpected.

Suddenly in mid-sentence, tears began to roll down my face. I can't remember the last time I cried for any reason. At first I was embarrassed. But then you comforted me telling me that it was okay. As you handed me your fine linen handkerchief, you said that something deep in me had been touched and to keep talking. You were right.

As I wiped my eyes, you gently kept prodding me with questions. It was as if you knew my response to your questions even before you asked.

But the tears, they just kept coming. It was like a dam broke and years of a emotion began to flow. I didn't even know all this was there. It was not like my dad was a bad man or any thing like that. It is just as his son, I needed more from him than I suppose he could offer. He always worked hard with long hours. He was a good provider for our family. Dad got us through the hard times of the Great Depression and the Dust Bowl, but it caused him to be away from me frequently at a time in my life when I needed him most.

And in that moment at dinner, I realized I had been trying to figure out life all alone, by myself, until you came along. Oh my! What am I saying? I love my dad, but Mr. A I am now beginning to comprehend how you have been speaking into places inside me where my father has been missing.

In our conversation last night you helped me see the real purpose in writing my first letter to you. I was looking for answers to questions my dad had never answered. And, maybe he simply did not have any answers. Regardless Mr. A, I am staggered by you. For a man of your stature to pause your life, so you could speak into mine; well, it is more than I can fathom.

Needless to say, I was not worth much at work today. Not only am I physically tired, but I am emotionally wrung out in a good way. It is hard to describe. Oddly I feel cleansed, relaxed; like after a long hot bath. In fact, it seems as if a peacefulness has settled on me.

It could take months, maybe years to fully step into all that you have told me. But do know, you have launched me on a journey to find my truest self. I have decided to head into that 'fog' to explore the 'vista' of which I have only had glimpses.

I have decided that I want to live into the fullness of the man that I have been created to be. I want to know my deepest desires, and I want those deepest desires to inform my greatest dreams. And I want to pursue those dreams, regardless of where they take me.

There was one moment after we had dessert when we were sipping our coffee, and again you looked me in the eye and you said:

> *"Son, follow your heart for it is the truest part of you. It is more than your emotions or mind or attitude or soul. It is the sum of all that is you. It will guide you well, like a compass points north."*

Truer words were never spoken, but Mr. A, I really never got past your first word: 'son'. In that moment, something inside me felt restored. I felt that I had been found and I was no longer alone. I no longer have to figure it out all by myself. What a relief!

Your coming alongside me has been huge. Thank you so very much. No matter what happens, I want you to know I will never forget last night and please know that you have had a lasting impact on my life. I have begun rereading all of our correspondence. I suspect there is much more in those letters than I realize.

I want you to know, Mr. A, that I am full of emotion towards you. I realize that you are for me, and that is empowering. I will always be indebted to you.

Deeply grateful,

Max

back in Salina, Kansas

~ Sage Advice to Apply: Patterns to Disappointments ~

We have only the one letter from Max to Mr. A that details their dinner conversation. However, in the notes found among his letters, it seems that Mr. A was very impressed with Max's dream scale and his rooting out of other dreams through his disappointments.

So at dinner, he guided Max in discovering any other disappointments associated with any of his unrealized dreams both as a youth or in present day. In other words, those dreams that were less than an 8 - 10 on Max's scale.

First, Mr. A asked Max what were the hindrances to each dream. Then, he had Max tell him about the hopes he had for that dream. Next, Mr. A gently asked him to describe the loss or disappointment surrounding that unrealized dream.

Would you consider trying Mr. A's approach for yourself?

‣ Select the most meaningful unrealized dreams from your lists as a youth and present day.

‣ Write down the dream and below it describe any hindrances that kept you from realizing that dream.

‣ Considering the hindrances to your dream, what were your hopes that the hindrances prevented you from realizing?

‣ Now, in this flow of dream, hindrances, and lost hopes; describe any loss or disappointments you experienced.

‣ Take your time and do this for each of your meaningful, unrealized dreams.

For Max, a pattern emerged to his disappointments that was not evident on the surface of his life. This disappointment pattern began to reveal how and why he hesitated in pursuing larger dreams and in fact had settled for smaller dreams.

For example Max gained clarity on why he had settled on the dream to become a manager as a part of another person's vision, rather than pursue his own entrepreneurial desire.

▸ Is there a pattern or common thread to your disappointments? Write down any observations you may have, especially if they relate to any type of entrepreneurial hopes.

Gathering Storm Clouds

Tuesday, November 25, 1941

Dear Max:

Your words are much too kind and generous towards me. For I have many shortcomings and faults which you will discover, if you are around me for any length of time. However, I am elated with your decision to risk all and begin a quest to discover what is most true about you. I am willing to assist you in any way I can.

From our conversation you know that I have experienced many disappointments in my life, despite my successes. Never forget what I told you: *"As the signers of the Declaration of Independence relied on Divine Providence, so have I"*. And, it has made all the difference. For I have experienced much healing and freedom from my disappointments.

I am incomparable to my former self. For I no longer live out of disappointment, instead I am living into the fullness of who I am truly intended to be. *It has been worth my life to now live without pretense.* Consequently, I am more alive than ever, even while negotiating the difficulties of this world.

Knowing that you benefited so much from our time together lifts my spirit, especially as the dark storm clouds of war gather around our country. As I shared at dinner, I am deeply concerned about the war expanding in Europe. My sources tell me, that we may only be weeks away from being drawn into the conflict with Germany. At present, our country is divided, but the nation cannot remain on the sidelines of history, forever.

I speak of this, Max, because this war is both real and illustrative. We live in a broken world. Bad things do happen. Like the Nazis, evil is intent on the destruction of all that is good. It will stop at nothing less than total domination. Similarly, evil assaults our dreams, our desires, and it especially assaults the truest things about us. This enemy of good strategizes that if one can be kept from living into their true purpose, then that person will never significantly impact the world for the better.

It would be like the Nazis convincing Great Britain to surrender, even before a shot has been fired. And, do not think they have not tried. It takes great resolve to resist succumbing to this kind of internal pressure, as evidenced by Mr. Churchill rallying England.

Max, imagine that as you pursue your desire to become an entrepreneur, evil assails that desire and shuts you down, so instead you settle: living a 'safe and predictable' life. What has the world lost? Some great service? Some revolutionary new product? Some life-saving device? We will never know.

There is something much more far-reaching occurring than meets the eye. Life is hard. Good is opposed. Finding freedom from your disappointments is a fight. Pursuing your dreams and desires is entering a battle.

Similar to the storm clouds of war that are gathering around our country, there could be storm clouds of a different kind of battle gathering around you. As you are receiving fresh insights and tastes of new found freedoms, remain alert. You will encounter setbacks. Keep up your defenses. Stay focused on your journey. Resist any opposition. Even one of the wisest and richest men who ever lived knew these truths. King Solomon's advice was *"Above all else guard the sum of whom you* are (i.e. what is most true about you) *for it is the well-spring of life."*

Max, let nothing thwart you from your pursuit of living into your true self. Do not allow the threat of war against our country discourage or dissuade you from this journey you have begun. Yes, it may be hard, but well worth the rewards. Success on a journey of this kind will exceed the abilities of your own self efforts. So, remember The Founders reliance on Divine Providence. Do the same.

If war happens with Germany, then consider it another assault to overcome on your quest to live authentically. Do not be dismayed by these unfolding events, Max.

For as Thanksgiving Day approaches, remember this from the October 3, 1863 proclamation President Lincoln made in the midst of the bloody Civil War:

> *"The year that is drawing towards its close, has been filled with the blessings of fruitful fields and healthful skies.*
>
> *To these bounties, which are so constantly enjoyed that we are prone to forget the source from which they come, others have been added, which are of so extraordinary a nature, that they cannot fail to penetrate and soften even the heart which is habitually insensible to the ever watchful providence of Almighty God."*

He set aside the last Thursday of November as a day of *"Thanksgiving and Praise"* in the midst of a great war. And so, Max, I wish you and your family a very Happy Thanksgiving!

Affectionately,

Mr. A

New York City

Pearl Harbor

Monday, December 8, 1941

Dear Max:

I simply had to write you since the Japanese suddenly attacked Pearl Harbor yesterday morning. Like the rest of the nation I am shocked by the surprise and ferocity of this assault against us on American soil. Today, in his address to the joint session of Congress, President Roosevelt summed it up perfectly:

"Yesterday, December 7, 1941, a date which will live in infamy...".

This was not at all what I was contemplating in my last letter when I wrote of the storm clouds of war approaching. Already I am hearing of the galvanizing effect this is having on the country. I am certain now that we will be at war with both Japan and Germany in a matter of weeks, if not days.

Steel yourself. Make yourself ready. For you are certainly one of those men that your country will call on to serve. I am glad we have had these few months of correspondence. Much will change for you, but you are ready in ways you may not even realize.

Max, no matter what happens, never forsake your quest. Never forget your journey. No matter the cost, where ever you may find yourself: live into the truest part of you, your authentic self.

And please, keep me up to date on all that is happening with you.

Your friend,

Mr. A

New York City

A World Upside-down

Friday, December 12, 1941

Dear Mr. A:

Last Sunday, I had started writing a letter to you when I heard the news of the Japanese attack on Pearl Harbor. Instantly, I experienced a flood of emotions: anger, fear, sadness. Unexpectedly tears began to well up in my eyes, but I quickly wiped them away.

Ever since our dinner I seem to feel more feelings, if that makes any sense. It is very confusing to me. I think my emotions were tied to fear this time, because everything felt out of control. With the news of Pearl Harbor I knew my life was about to change, so I stopped writing to regain some perspective.

Seeking support, I have been rereading your letter of November 25th and my notes about what we discussed at dinner. What has really struck me is your suggestion how my journey could be opposed. Both in that letter and at dinner when you talked about evil, I thought your descriptions were overblown. I assumed you were probably exaggerating to capture my attention.

Frankly Mr. A, you are not the first to use a 'war metaphor' with me. To be honest that metaphor makes me uncomfortable because of the violent imagery it connotes. I think a war metaphor may work for older generations because of The Great War, as it is closer to their reality. But, it feels outdated to me and my generation.

I had been thinking: *hasn't society moved beyond war analogies?* Is there some non-violent metaphor that could convey the same point? After all, war requires the victor to conquer, dominate, kill, destroy, etc., and that does not seem true to who I am.

However, sometime between the Pearl Harbor attack, receiving your December 7th letter, and reviewing your November 25th letter alongside my journal notes, it dawned on me that you may not be speaking in a metaphor. In fact, maybe you truly believe there is warfare headed my way. Maybe from Japan? or Germany? or some other unseen opposition?

I agree that this adventure to find authenticity is full of risk and the outcome is unknown, but *the idea that it could be opposed had never occurred to me.* I agree that evil is real. Here again, I guess I simply thought that evil just happened randomly. The idea that evil could be intentionally directed at me, seeking to dominate and destroy me, is a new possibility for me to consider.

To test your idea, I began to recall some older men that I know who once had big dreams. In general, it seems over the years they lost heart for their ideas. The stories they tell reflect that. In fact, they have settled into routines of life far from those dreams. Now that I think about it, they seem to just go through the motions of living, and I feel sad for them.

Mr. A, are you suggesting that evil possibly opposed their dreams and has had some affect on them? That evil *actually knocked them out* from having the impact living into their true self was designed to have without them ever realizing it?

Summarizing the latest news: the Japanese have attacked Pearl Harbor, while Germany continues its invasion of the Soviet Union. Soldiers and citizens are are being killed and captured. *The message of the enemy is do not resist, your doom is certain.* The Axis powers are seeking world domination and the end to life as we know it, even here in the United States.

I am beginning to understand that resistance costs. Pursuit of freedom costs. Doing nothing could cost us everything, like these older men living aimless lives, or much worse!

To fully live into the people (the nation) we were created to be, we must act, as one. Suddenly, your 'war metaphor' is quickly becoming my reality.

I know I will be joining my fellow countrymen and going to war. So Mr. A, how do I continue my journey for authenticity, pursuing my dreams and desires, while everything around me is changing? Just as I was receiving a bit of clarity, my world feels like it has been turned upside down!

Thank you for your letters, your words are an enormous encouragement to me. I feel like events may be happening quickly. Pray for me.

I will stay in touch, thanks for your friendship.

> Your friend,
>
> *Max*
>
> Salina, Kansas (for now)

Golden Opportunity

Monday, December 22, 1941

Dear Max:

Thank you for the Christmas card and letter. Even though the country is moving quickly towards a war footing, it is good for all of us to pause and celebrate Christmas. A season of hope for a world that is in desperate need of hope; now, more than ever.

Max, I am greatly impressed by your resoluteness to pursue the truest things about you, face your disappointments and continue to dream knowing that you may soon be going to war.

Your question to me reflects your intentionality: "...how do I continue my journey for authenticity, pursuing my dreams and desires, while everything around me is changing?"

This is a journey of self, but not a selfish journey. Ultimately, this journey could lead to impacting your world for a good greater than yourself. And it bears repeating, the best way to become an effective transformative force is living into your authentic self, regardless of your circumstance.

Max, there is a high probability that you may soon be thrust into situations beyond your control. In the military there is order and discipline and few individual rights. The battlefield to which you may go is a place of confusion, desolation and horror. The people around you may or may not share your same convictions or desires. However, none of that needs to deter your quest, unless you allow it. The basic question to which you seek an answer is, "Who am I?"

A practical answer to your question would be to observe yourself in the various circumstances.

How are you responding to your surroundings and the
actions of others around you? What are you thinking
about? What are you feeling? What does your reaction say

about you? What clues about your disappointments and desires are being revealed? What do you hear the deepest part of you telling yourself?

Max, your war experience could be a debilitating season or a golden opportunity. So, what do I mean by that statement?

I once knew a man who was strongly encouraged into military service. He was reluctant to join, but volunteered anyway. During the first few months he was miserable, because he failed to accept the new order and discipline to which he had joined.

Inwardly, he resisted and reacted, although outwardly he tried to appear willing. His poor attitude could not remain hidden and seeped out regardless of his best efforts to contain it. It negatively impacted his relationship with some of those men around him, even affecting his future advancement.

What he failed to realize at the time was that this military experience was a golden opportunity to begin sorting out his disappointments and begin healing, instead he became self protective and defensive. Unbeknownst to him, the tough times were touching old hurts in the deep places of his soul. *Until the unresolved became resolved, he could never begin living into his authentic self.*

Eventually, he adjusted and developed a coping style that salvaged most relationships and enable him to gain some advancement. However, he never experienced the golden opportunity of resolving and healing past disappointments, nor did he fully realize his potential while in the service.

Max, I know of what I write, for that man was me. It would take much larger disappointments in my life to bring me through to finding my authentic self. Oh how I wish I knew what I know today; how much better I could have been! However, I do not live with regrets, rather a deep gratitude for the authenticity in which I now experience. For you see, few men ever discover these great treasures.

Since we have no idea what may lie ahead for you, my hope and prayer is that you will face the future well, gaining much along the way. What evil may intend for your destruction, know that there is a greater good that can overcome it.

I hope my story of failures will inspire you. As you requested, I am praying for you.

Merry Christmas!

Mr. A

New York City

Carpe Diem

Tuesday, January 6, 1942

Dear Mr. A:

My family and I have enjoyed celebrating Christmas together, plus ringing in the New Year, regardless of what the future may hold. Events are moving quickly and the buzz in Salina is all about which young men are enlisting in the military.

Your military experience story stirred me deeply and rather than waiting for events to unfold on me, I decided to take the initiative and see what options I might have. Yesterday, I went downtown and spoke to the local Army recruiter. He interviewed me, had me take some kind of test and in less than hour he offered me a slot in the next Officer Candidates School (OCS). It was one of those moments that I miraculously had the presence to realize that if I didn't seize the day, the opportunity could be lost forever.

So Mr. A, I accepted the offer. The Army has recruited me to be a Second Lieutenant in the Tank Corps. Apparently, my education and experience make me an ideal officer candidate. I am headed off to OCS soon. From there I go to tank school and then begin training with my unit. Assuming that we are still at war, I will be shipped out to combat, somewhere.

My head is spinning. These are all the details that I know. Even though the paperwork and orders are being drawn up, the recruiter told me: "...any of this could change at any time, welcome to the Army son!" There was that word again, 'son'. Again, I felt emotions but thankfully I was able to contain them!

Now I see how one turn of events can deeply impact a person's dreams, maybe forever. In less than a month the course of my life has dramatically changed, as has the course of our nation. My life is not my own, anymore. I now serve at the pleasure of the President for an army fighting in places that I have never even heard of.

The last month feels like a blur. I only wish I was more centered about who I truly am. To that end, I started a list of the most authentic things I know about myself. But it is hard to see things clearly, especially right now in the midst of all the drama in my life due to the war. So, I decided to obtain the help of a few people who know me well. Here is my idea:

I have carefully selected six friends and three family members who have known me at different times of my life. I am asking them all the same question:

"What would you say are the most authentic, truest, distinct things about me? When you think of me what positive characteristics or strengths come to mind?"

My plan is to summarize each response into several characteristics. Then identify the top 3 to 5 most recurring characteristics from all the responses. Next, I will compare the summarized list to mine, and try to settle on my final top 3 to 5 characteristics.

I imagine this final list will provide me an objective starting point of what is most true about me. My intention is to lean into those top characteristics and operate from them in the myriad of real-life circumstances I am about to face.

So Mr. A, I have two questions for you: First, how does my process sound to you? And second, would you be the first to answer my authentic questions and send me your list of characteristics you believe best describe me?

Thank you again for your friendship and all your insights and encouragements you have given me. I remember that you told me at dinner how you had the last sentence from the Declaration of Independence framed and hanging by the door of your office to remind you that those brave men were *"...guided by Divine*

Providence". Honestly, I am afraid of what lies ahead, but like our founders I, too, am trusting Divine Providence to guide me.

My guess is that I will be leaving Salina in a few weeks for OCS. I will keep you posted on my address. Please know, your letters always refresh and inspire me.

You have blessed me tremendously; and I thank you from the bottom of my heart.

Your friend,

Max

Salina, Kansas (for a little longer)

You Have What It Takes!

Wednesday, January 14, 1942

My dearest Max:

You are a man who has what it takes! Do not doubt yourself. Your actions in the moment of choice offered by the Army Recruitment Officer demonstrate your lucidity and intentionality. I applaud you. For you now have a much coveted officer slot in Officer Candidates School. Well done in seizing the day. Carpe Diem!

Allow me to further say, that for you to recognize the opportunity as it was offered and to seize it in the moment is a measure of how far you have come in a very short period of time. Do you think that you would have reacted with as much confidence six months ago?

As to your authenticity process Max, it is brilliant in its simplicity. By gathering observations from others who have known you personally in different phases of your life is both straightforward and uncomplicated. Your questions should elicit considerable insights. I particularly like the distillation of the lists from each person. Identifying similar occurring characteristics will be noteworthy, as each person has differing perspectives on you.

I imagine your final list will describe you well, providing healthy indicators of what is most authentic about you. Even more significant, may be limiting your list to the top three to five characteristics. Such a short list should be easy to remember, allowing you to begin observing how true they are for you.

I consider it an honor that you would want my opinion to your questions, since we have known each other for a short time and have met only once. Per your questions and in no particular order, my observations about your most authentic attributes are:

- You are full of ideas and vision.
- You are a man of interpersonal relationships and not afraid of interdependence with others.
- You are bold, seize opportunity, pursuing your future through self-initiation.
- You are reflective and thoughtful: you think about what you are thinking about.
- You are teachable.
- You are a leader, preferring to chart the course instead of managing the situation.
- You are honest, full of integrity, and loyal.
- You are an entrepreneur in the truest sense of the word: willing to take risks and willing to accept responsibility.
- You are a good communicator.

Max, as you head off into the unknown, I would encourage you to invest in what is truly lasting and not be tempted by what can disappear quickly. Influence, power, financial success, etc.; all fade quickly. As you have noted, a turn of events like Pearl Harbor can change everything.

So, what is indubitably lasting?

Remain true to yourself. Live without pretense. Despite my worldly success, my greatest treasures are those with whom I enjoy a deep and true relationship. Life is a precious gift. Cherish it.

Max, your adventurous journey continues, albeit in a completely unexpected direction. You are well equipped for what lies ahead. You are on my heart and in my thoughts and prayers.

Again I declare to you, Max North: "You have what it takes!" Godspeed to you, my dear friend.

Affectionately,

Mr. A

New York City

~ Sage Advice to Apply: Discovering your Authenticity ~

Mr. A described Max's activity to help him discover what was most authentic and distinctive about himself as *"brilliant in its simplicity"*.

So, would you consider applying Max's process to yourself?

‣ Brainstorm a list of characteristics and strengths that are the most authentic about you. List all that you can. Then circle the top 3 - 5.

‣ Select 5 - 10 friends and family members. It is best for each of them to have a different perspective of you: from various times in your life, assorted levels of relationship, and differing settings. For example: a spouse, best friend, a person from work (co-worker, boss, subordinate), family members (a sibling, parent, even an adult child) a close friend(s) from the past (like college or high school) that may not be currently active in your life, friends that experience you in other settings (i.e., a club, place of worship, sports team, weekly group, etc.).

Communicate with them in writing. Explain to them that you are following an entrepreneurial process and are surveying several close friends to help you identify what is truest and most distinctive about you.

Ask them a question like:

> *"When you think of me, what are the top 3 - 5 most authentic, distinctive characteristics and/or strengths that come to your mind that you think best describe me?"*

or as Max wrote his friends and family:

> *"What would you say are the most authentic, truest, distinct things about me? When you think of me what positive*

characteristics or strengths come to mind?"

[This can be a very encouraging process. Rarely will you receive negative descriptors, if you do, it is best to ignore them for the purposes of this process.]

- Summarize the descriptions you receive from each person into a one word characteristic or a very short phrase. Circle the ones that appear on multiple lists. The ones with the most circles probably belong in your top 3 - 5 of what others say about you.

- Compare this list to your list. Between the 2 lists, which 3 - 5 characteristics seem the most true?

- Write your final *truest characteristics list* by choosing your top 3 - 5 most authentic and distinctive characteristics from these 2 lists. Begin to observe how you operate from these characteristics and test how true they are about you. Refine the list, as you progress with greater insights.

~ Sage Advice to Apply: Your Entrepreneurial Bent ~

Mr. A advised Max after his return from the war to consider several questions to help reconnect him to his original entrepreneurial desires. However, it would be great for you to begin considering them now.

These questions will help pull together all your previous work from the Sage Advice Applications and further your self-discovery of the entrepreneurial endeavor most suited for you to pursue.

With your dream list and final truest characteristics list, begin brainstorming around these questions:

▸ *Reflect on your strongest desires, dreams, and hopes. What entrepreneurial related desires can you observe?*

▸ *In regards to your truest characteristics, what entrepreneurial qualities do you observe about yourself?*

▸ *What is your entrepreneurial bent?* (That is your natural entrepreneurial inclination or talent.)

Now step back and reflect on all your Sage Advice answers and the observations from others about what is most true about you:

▸ *Considering your list of entrepreneurial desires, brainstorm what entrepreneurial endeavors could be most suitable for you to pursue?*

▸ *Or in other words, what do you dream / desire your entrepreneurial endeavor could be?* (List some possibilities.)

▸ *Pick one endeavor and describe what it is. What experience it could create for you and others.*

Plan on revisiting and refining these answers, as you follow more of Mr. A's guidance in Part Two and Three.

PART TWO: Post-War Creative Disruption

~ the intervening war years ~

During World War II the letters between Max and Mr. A were few and far between. Their correspondence became more regular after the war ends in 1945 and Max's return to Salina.

The few letters that were exchanged in the intervening years have been discovered tucked into various journals that Max tried to keep during the war. He reveals very little in these letters. Records show that Max completed Officer Candidate School, received his commission as a 2nd Lieutenant and was assigned to the 2nd Armored Division stationed at Fort Benning, Georgia.

He became a tank commander while in Africa serving under General George S. Patton. Later, he would join the 3rd Army on Patton's sweep through France into Germany. Without question, Max served honorably and was highly decorated for his time in the military.

Throughout World War II Max received multiple battlefield promotions. When the war ended he had achieved the rank of Lt. Colonel and was serving on a general's staff in a full bird colonel's role. Based on the news accounts of the period, Max returned to Salina quite the war hero.

Although his notes are irregular, a picture emerges that Max was able to live more and more into his true identity which helped him immensely during the atrocities of war. It also contributed to his promotions and expanded leadership roles and responsibilities.

From his later letters, it is evident that the war deeply shaped him and affected the future course of his life; especially, his encounter with the poverty and human deprivation in Africa. At times, it seems it was more than he could bear, even in later years.

Despite all his successes in the Army, Max knew that one of the truest things about him was not soldiering. Like so many others who faithfully served their country in the Second World War, he would leave the Army and reenter private life.

The letters we found begin again with Mr. A writing Max after Victory in Europe Day. Max is still stationed in Europe helping the Army transition to the post-war effort.

By the time this collection of letters ends, Mr. A has brilliantly helped Max focus his passions! And perhaps helped you *focus your passions*, as well.

Creativity from Disruption

Saturday, June 30, 1945

My dear Max:

A well-connected friend of mine at the Pentagon gave me this address for you and suggested that you might be shipping out soon. I am hoping you receive this letter before sailing for New York City. To be honest, this is actually three letters in one, hence its length.

I was also informed that you have distinguished yourself in numerous ways during the war, even being decorated by General Patton, himself! Based on my friend's reports a picture emerges that you attained great victories leading men into battle by engaging the enemy with intense fortitude, while enduring times of considerable hardship.

Max, I am so proud of you! I am in awe of the great courage and leadership you have demonstrated during the war.

You, along with all the soldiers of the Allied forces, have suffered greatly for the cause of freedom, many sacrificing their own lives. I can only imagine the personal toll this has cost you. Please know, my friend, that I along with the entire nation are eternally grateful for your sacrifice, and the sacrifice of every soldier to save us from the tyranny and oppression of the Axis powers.

So, hear these words: *"Well done, Colonel Max North!"*. My love and admiration towards you knows no bounds! Thus, I am compelled to demonstrate to you my immense gratitude by extending to you my continued friendship and love.

In addition, you have my hospitality while you are in New York City. I insist you stay with me and allow me to take care of your every need. You have no choice in this matter, Colonel! Am I making myself clear!?! Even as I write this in a stern tone, I am

61

smiling because I know how reticent you are to accept charity.

~ 3 letters in 1 ~

So in the spirit of that charity, which is my love towards you, allow me to share some thoughts that may

~ help you process your war experiences,

~ begin your integration back into civilian life,

~ and even stir those pre-war entrepreneurial dreams of yours.

Please know Max, that I write these words with the greatest humility having never experienced the battlefield, myself. But, of this I am certain: even though you are returning home a decorated war hero, no man experiences the theater of war without being deeply affected, including you.

My aspiration is that you will have time to ponder these ideas prior to your departure and during your transatlantic voyage. To that end, I have arranged this letter in sections for ease of reading and reference.

What follows are some of my most treasured ideas on creativity and entrepreneurism.

~ The colossal disruption of the battlefield ~

Max, has it occurred to you that you have experienced more than a lifetime of colossal disruptions? Outside of war, few ever know such disruptions. Any single aspect of the horrors of war would deeply disrupt anyone: the pressures and fears, the stresses of leadership, enduring the pain and suffering, the deprivations, the loss of dear brothers in arms, witnessing mass suffering and death. Even, victories can disrupt. But compressing all of that and more into a few years makes me wonder if at times it seems overpowering?

I must confess that I am most unacquainted with these kinds of war experience related disruptions; however, I have experienced other types of life altering disruptions. If you will indulge me, I would like to share some ideas on disruption and how it can be positively transforming, and not debilitating.

~ Creating through disruption ~

Are you familiar with the story of Brunelleschi's egg? If not, read on.

By the early 1400's the Santa Maria del Fiore Cathedral (Il Duomo) in Florence, Italy had remained unfinished for almost a century. At that time it was the largest cathedral in the world, except no one had devised a way to construct a dome over its vast nave. Thus, what was intended to be the glory of Florence was its shame.

In 1420 the merchants and leaders of the city assembled the greatest architects and artists in the known world to pit their designs for a dome against each other. According to Giorgio Vasari, the Florentine 16th century historian, Filippo Brunelleschi *"declared that he could make a vaulted roof without much wood, without pillars or supports, and with little expense of arches."* Filippo's idea was roundly mocked and all said he spoke like a madman.

The secret to understanding Filippo's confidence is that years earlier he had gone to Rome and studied the ancient buildings, especially their arches and domes. In the year prior to the competition he particularly focused on the Pantheon. For you see, Filippo believed that no one, but himself could design the dome.

Ah, Max, here is a man who was truly an entrepreneur! He could see what no one else could, and he had the confidence of faith to build it! One might even posit that this is what Filippo believed he was intended for, while on this earth.

According to Vasari, Brunelleschi was not to be thwarted by the first rejection, so he armed himself with patience and parlayed with individual council members to reposition himself. His politicking, another secret of entrepreneurs, paid off in a second meeting of the council to dispute the matter.

Vasari described the meeting as follows:

> *"The other architects desired that Filippo would tell all his mind and show his model. This he would not do, but made a proposal that the building of the cupola should be given to him who could make an egg stand firmly on the smooth marble, for by doing this he would show his skill. And an egg being brought, all the masters tried to make it stand upright, but none found the way. And when they bade Filippo set it up, he took it, and striking it on the marble made it stand. And the architects murmured, saying that they could have done that; but Filippo replied laughing that they could have built the cupola, too, if they had seen his model and designs. So it was resolved that the charge of the work should be entrusted to him."*

~ Disruptive creativity ~

This story has been used to illustrate innovation and discovery of new ideas, but I believe it reveals more. What seemed an impossible problem, in hindsight was creatively solved in a disruptive way. I believe that disruptive creativity, such as this, flows from disruption in life.

Over the course of the 16 years required to build the dome, there were numerous other disruptions that were solved by Filippo's further innovations of pulleys, cranes, a small cafe up top, and clever leadership techniques.

So, was there disruption in Filippo's life? Unfortunately, not much is known. He was the second born child, trained to be a civil servant like his father educated in literature and mathematics. Instead of following his father, he pursued his artistic passions going from master goldsmith to working in bronze, sculpture, then architecture and mechanical engineering. His impact on the Renaissance is undisputed.

Such diversity of study and accomplishment strongly suggest a life of disruption. We know he suffered great disappointment on occasion and he was clearly a reflective man. Imagine living Filippo's life of great innovation and creativity and passion, one can not help but feel disruption.

As a touch of irony, notice the egg shaped quality to Brunelleschi's dome built for this domeless cathedral which had been disrupting Florence for a century. Or, maybe this was not irony, at all. Truly this genius knew a thing or two about creativity flowing out of disruption.

~ Disruption is inevitable ~

Throughout our lifetimes all of us will encounter disruptions of some kind. Loss of loved ones, disease, divorce, violence, war, natural or man made disasters are just a few of the countless life altering disruptions mortals experience on this earth.

Our hope for that ideal life is shattered by disruption. Life as we once knew it has been altered and we are forever changed. And with great disruption there is great emotion: perhaps anger, sorrow and grief, fear, hurt and pain, and loss, oh yes, there is often much loss.

Each of us has a choice as to how we will allow disruption to affect us. Will we be bitter? Will we forgive? Will we be angry? Will we love? How will we respond?

Whether we believe it or not, we do have a choice. Most would agree that one could respond either positively or negatively.

But, I believe that there is another kind of response: a creative response. Similar to Filippo, I have observed that many inventions, and in fact many entrepreneurial endeavors, have come through disruption of one degree or another.

As Plato wrote in the Republic, *"...and yet a true creator is necessity, which is the mother of our invention."* Or, as more commonly stated: *"Necessity is the mother of all invention"*. Necessities spring from lack or losses. And, losses can be more or less disruptive depending on their severity.

~ How does creativity flow from disruption? ~

While experiencing disruption we can become disoriented, even temporarily losing the context of our life, typically commensurate to the degree of disruption. Thus in this loss of context, we are no longer bound to the customary constraints and boundaries within which we typically live, because they no longer exist. Paradoxically, that is why there is freedom to create after a disruption.

Therefore, when we realize, i.e. accept that life has changed, and that there is no going back to the way things were; we are at the moment of decision.

We can choose to live creatively out of the disruption,
or not.

As there are degrees of disruptions, so there are proportional degrees of creative responses. Allow me to explain.

~ Gentle disruptions are manageable ~

Max, consider your life before your war experience. Your life's context was the small town of Salina, Kansas. Friends, family, church, work, play were all elements of your story and your daily routine; thereby creating a sense of predictability and security.

Yet, even in this idyllic setting, something disrupted you or at the very least stirred you to write a letter to me. That letter did not fit the context of your life. The very fact I even responded to your letter was disrupting.

In truth, the whole of our correspondence has had a disruptive effect: propelling you in new directions beyond the context of your life. Nevertheless, your life in Salina remained a distinct point of reference. So, let us refer to this as a gentle disruption, to wit a disruption that is manageable.

Consider a picture of what I mean by a gentle disruption. Living your life in Salina is analogous to living in your house. There are rooms and halls and walls and doors which frame the house and direct where one can go and not go, similar to the various parameters of our day to day living.

Therefore, stepping out of the context of your daily life, is like leaving your house and going out to the backyard to camp out and cook where you might feel a degree of disruption or unpredictability. But even though you are outside of your house you are living in reference to the context of your house, trees and property outlined by fences. You can quickly end the disruption by going back into the house.

In daily life this might be the equivalent of going on some adventurous trip. In most cases, if it begins to feel too disruptive then all one must do is simply end the trip and return home. However, even in those moments of unpredictability and disruption, there is an undercurrent of exhilaration, and yes, creativity!

~ Harsher disruptions ~

Now imagine high winds or even a tornado blowing through your neighborhood that flatten all the fences, rip off a few roofs, and uproots some trees. As you emerge from your home the devastation is disorienting because what was once there is now gone. The boundaries of fences and familiarity of certain trees have vanished. However, there is still a reference point, your home oriented to the other homes in the neighborhood, even though trees are gone and property lines blend together.

Harsher disruptions can foster greater creativity. As in this case, there is an opportunity to redesign the look and feel of the neighborhood, even though the homes remain. In other words, as more reference points are disrupted; the greater the opportunity for more creativity, because there is less context to confine our imagination.

~ Colossal disruptions ~

For the sake of comparison, let us say that a massive tornado swept through Salina obliterating not only your home, but the entire neighborhood and most of the town. Nothing is recognizable, even whole streets are either ripped up or covered over by dirt and debris. Even though no life was lost, this is devastation on an unimaginable scale. Any possible reference points are gone, except map coordinates that can identify where the town was once located.

Colossal disruptions offer the opportunity for the greatest creativity because there are no reference points. However, the greater the disruption the more difficult it is to choose a creative response, as it is human nature to succumb to such extreme, heartbreaking loss and devastation. *One must battle to create after disruption.*

Nature illustrates this very concept. For after a devastating forest fire, the land will burst forth with new flowers and plants and trees, some that have never been seen in that area. Or consider a monstrous volcanic eruption where lava and volcanic ash cover vast areas. Within a few years new vegetation will fill the landscape more dense and varied than ever before.

Max remember this: *the more reference points we lose, the greater the occasion to become an all new creation.* This is the way the world works. It is built into its design.

Even Filippo had at the most only one reference point, the base wall of the cathedral upon which to construct a dome. However, above the wall was only air, nothingness. Thus, with virtually no reference points, he created the largest masonry dome the world has ever seen.

This is why none of the greatest creators in Florence could make the egg stand on its end. They limited their creativity by relying on the egg as a reference point. Filippo started with no reference point, and devised the solution of cracking the end of the egg on the marble to make it stand.

~ How to experience great creativity ~

Max, may I suggest that the disruption of the war in your life may be on the scale of an entire city being wiped away. Like Filippo with only the cathedral wall, you may have at best, only one reference point left in your life: Salina, Kansas. Life will never be the same for you. On the outside you may appear unchanged to the casual observer, but on the inside your soul and spirit have suffered a colossal disruption.

Now, is a moment of great opportunity, because from this colossal disruption, great creativity can burst forth. However, to experience great creativity you must embrace the disorientation of all your pain and loss. So, allow yourself the time and space to absorb the disruption you have experienced, including the complicated mix of emotions of great loss alongside great victory.

Proceed slowly as you reenter civilian life. There is no hurry.

Restoration of this kind takes as long as it needs, irrespective of other people's opinions. Bear in mind that you need as long as you need, no more and no less!

Best of all Max, true healing is available for all the hurt and pain associated with the disruption. The memory remains, and of course the losses, but the pain is drained away because the wounds are healed. It is most amazing! We do not forget whoever or whatever we lost; but we are restored. In fact, in some ways we are made new.

That is why *time does NOT heal*, as the old saying declares: *"time heals all wounds"*. In and of itself time can prolong the pain of disruptions which can settle into a long lasting bitterness or worse, sometimes with physical consequences.

Only healing heals, I know personally of what I speak!

Finally, there is something curious about healed disruptive events in our lives. We can always go back to them in our imagination years later. We can travel back to that moment of few reference points and create again. Those awful places can actually become wells of creativity.

So, stay with this disruption and pain, seek healing and it will be added to you. And know the creative benefit of this colossal disruption will always remain for you to revisit and draw from.

~ What path now? ~

So, how does one begin to move forward into creativity?

Well first, please know that it is human nature after disruptions to ask: *"why?"*. I can assure you from my personal experiences that this question will never lead you to creative choices. Even if the question were completely answered, it will lead nowhere, not even to more understanding.

Instead, ask yourself this question: *"what now?"* or more precisely, *"what path now?"*. It will begin releasing great creativity.

For this question begs one to look up and outward towards the horizon of their desires which begins to release one's imagination. The question "why?" turns one inward seeking explanations that they incorrectly hope will heal.

Such are my words to you, Max: embrace the pain, seek healing, and begin asking: "what path now?".

Finally Max, whereas virtually every American sincerely appreciates your sacrifices and service; few will understand the disruptions you are experiencing. Please allow yourself time to heal physically, emotionally, and spiritually. To this end, I will support you and encourage you in every way I know how.

When you arrive in New York City, look for me, as I will be eagerly awaiting you on the quay! I have made arrangements for you to stay with me at my apartment in Manhattan as long as you like. Furthermore, my staff have standing instructions that they are at your disposal for anything you may need. Max, words can not express how much I look forward to our reunion!

May your travels be safe and your journey easy,

Mr. A

New York City

HISTORICAL NOTE:

Mr. A's *"creative disruption"* letter was cutting edge thinking for the 1940's. It would not be until the late 1960's that managerial consultants first introduced the phrase, *"thinking outside the box"*, as way to describe creative thinking.

It is speculated that "the box" was based on the nine dot puzzle devised by Sam Loyd and introduced in his book of puzzles in 1914. The origins of Loyd's nine dot puzzle is believed to be sourced in the Egg of Columbus.

According to the story, Columbus was confronted by some Spanish nobles that the discovery of America was destined to occur sooner or later, and in reality was no great feat. To disprove this notion, Columbus challenged the men to stand an egg on its end. They all failed. He then gently broke the end of the egg, thereby standing it on end. In so doing Columbus illustrated that once an undertaking has been achieved, then anyone can see how to do it.

If the Columbus story is true, it occurred at least 70 years after Brunelleschi cracked his egg. Perhaps Columbus had heard of Brunelleschi's story, since his home in Genoa is some 200 kilometers northwest of Florence.

So, how might Mr. A react to the phrase:

"thinking outside the box"?

One can only speculate. However, based on this letter it is easy to imagine Mr. A asking:

"How is thinking outside the box, thinking the most creatively? After all, there is still a box that is the reference point."

In fact, he might add with a sly grin, that the truly creative would ask:

"What box?"

Then, wildly create with no constraints of reference points!

My Return

Monday, July 30, 1945

Dear Mr. A:

What a surprise and joy to hear from you! I am very impressed that you were able to track me down and have a letter delivered to me. Over the last few years I would receive a letter from you, precisely when I needed it most, and this one is no exception.

I have wondered how many letters you may have written for every letter I actually received. Thank you for your faithful friendship. It means the world to me.

I am to ship out on Thursday from France to New York City. I would very much enjoy spending time with you before I head on to Salina. In fact, I may need a little help making those arrangements, as I am not sure the Army has that leg of my travels worked out.

Mr. A, your perspective on creative disruption and my war experiences is giving me much to think about. Plus, I am intrigued and enlightened by the story of Filippo Brunelleschi.

So much has happened that it is hard for me to know where to begin. I tried to keep a journal, but my entries were sporadic. When I would record experiences, I would turn the page and not look back. Even now, I am not so sure I can read any of those pages. In spite of that, your letter does inspire me to begin opening my old journals and taking a look.

You are right about the pain the troops and I have suffered. But, I would hasten to add that there has been much joy, too! Many towns welcomed us as liberators with great celebrations while we marched and fought across Europe towards Germany. The people's reactions were immensely gratifying and healing.

I would like to forget all the bad stuff, remember the good moments, and just move on with my life. However, you have deeply challenged me with your words: *"Embrace the pain"*. Honestly, I am afraid of what that could dredge up. And that is saying a lot, because after all that I have been through, there is not much I am afraid of.

However, I do suffer the sudden and vivid remembering of a horrible event or a bad nightmare or even unexpected emotions that suddenly well up within me. All this is making it difficult to just "move on with my life".

Mr. A, do you have any idea how I can find some relief? You write of healing. Is that even possible? Can the creative disruption of which you speak really occur, even in the midst of all this?

Since V-E day, I have been very busy in helping wind down the war effort and preparing my troops to return home. So, I have coped by staying very busy and living one day at a time. But I am very tired, yet I am unsure of what may happen to me if I slow down.

Nevertheless, I am ready to return to the United States, and I look forward to seeing you. Perhaps, you will have some more "sage advice" for me. I could sure use some!

Your friend,

Max

Le Havre, France

~ Sage Advice to Apply: A Disruptive Reflection ~

Periodically, it is good to pause and reflect on our lives. Max does this through his letters to Mr. A. Other times, he journals his innermost thoughts, as we know from the journals we have found.

Just as Mr. A guides Max to delve back into his disruptions to seize creativity, so it is the same with this Sage Advice:

Write a disruptive reflection.

Suggestions:

‣ Find yourself a quiet, comfortable moment when you will not be interrupted.

‣ Take a blank sheet of paper or your journal to write down your reflections.

‣ Hint: It may be helpful to write your thoughts as a letter - like to Mr. A. Sometimes, by telling someone else our deeper thoughts it is easier to draw them out, even if it is a letter we will never send.

Write about a significant disruption in your own life and what resulted from it.

Answering these questions could help prompt your reflection:

‣ How did the disruption occur?

‣ What did the disruption remove from you life?

‣ Describe the affect of any suffering you may have experienced from the disruption.

‣ How have you responded? Would you put words to the range of emotions you experienced?

‣ How about forgiveness? And healing? What could those look

like or were like?

Like Max, it may be difficult to go back into a time of disruption, especially if there is grief or pain associated with it. That is ok. As, Mr. A knew it would be good for Max, so it will be good for you. Take your time. Be patient with yourself.

<u>Hint</u>: Where there is pain, typically there is unhealed hurt, even emotional hurt. If you are so inclined, invite Providence to meet you in that moment of disruption, to reveal his presence, and to heal you.

Once you are clear about the disruption, imagine yourself back in that moment. This is the moment when there are no "eggs" or "boxes" or "houses" to serve as reference points.

Reflect and answer these questions:

▸ What freedom(s) could you now live into as a result of that disruption, since you are no longer bound by any reference points. For example, freedom from a fear?, a person?, an action against you?, etc.

▸ Now, imagine living into that freedom: What could be your creative response? Your invention? Your entrepreneurial itch?

▸ Ask the question: *"What path now?"* (not *"why"*!) Write down any answers that pop into your head.

Once you have written your disruptive reflection, set it aside. Review it in a day or so, and make notes of any other observations, reactions and / or thoughts that may have occurred to you.

<u>One more hint</u>: Even with no reference points, you may be inclined to limit your reflection because of finances. After all, one must eat and keep a roof over their head. However, for purposes of this reflection do NOT allow any monetary needs to limit your creative response! *So, now what!?!*

Interlude in New York City

After Max set sail for the United States there is a three month gap in the correspondence between him and Mr. A. Curious about what may have transpired we searched for clues from any other journals or notes. We did discover several letters between Mr. A and Max's family, and we were able to piece together a partial timeline.

Records indicate that Max arrived in New York City on Tuesday, August 14, 1945 via the Marechal Joffre which had set sail from Le Havre, France about 12 days earlier. Somehow, Max was able to travel with elements of the 6th Armored Division.

It appears that Mr. A arranged for Max's family to come to New York City to welcome Max when he arrived. Based on some notes of Mr. A, Max was hospitalized for several weeks with severe exhaustion, some intestinal issues and other physical injuries that he had never mentioned.

On Sunday, September 2, 1945 Japan surrendered on the deck of U.S.S. Missouri. Celebrations of V-J Day broke out across the country and the world. The largest crowd gathered in Times Square in New York City. It is safe to assume that Max and his family went to Times Square and participated in the celebrations.

Upon the assurance of the doctors that Max was recovering well, his family returned to Salina. Max remained in New York and continued to convalesce after his hospital stay at Mr. A's home in the Hamptons on Long Island throughout September and most of October.

When it was declared that Saturday, October 27, 1945 would be Navy Day in New York City, Max decided to stay for the festivities surrounding the review of the Navy on the Hudson River and

President Truman's address in Central Park. He left for Salina the following Monday.

We have few details of what may have transpired between Mr. A and Max during his stay. However, every indication is that Mr. A took very good care of his friend, even providing him with some psychological post-war counseling. Something that was quite ahead of its time in dealing with those men returning from the battlefield. In today's parlance, Max suffered from post-traumatic stress disorder (PTSD).

After his time of recuperation in New York, Max would head home and return to private life. He would continue his recovery from his colossal disruption in Salina. The next letter we have is Max writing from the train, as he left New York City.

Thank You

Monday, October 29, 1945

Dear Mr. A:

As I ride the train back to Salina my heart is full of gratitude towards you for all the kindnesses you have shown me.

Thank you for insisting I stay in New York City to attend the Navy Day Celebrations. I was awed by the turnout of one million people to hear the President in Central Park and to feel their appreciation for all who have served in the wars against Germany and Japan. Truly this was as cathartic as all the other ways you have attended to my needs.

But later in the day, when you told me that you had a little surprise for me before I left The City; I could tell by the gleam in your eye you were up to something! I had no idea you were taking me to a private reception where you personally introduced me to President Truman!!!

Oh my, he was so kind and honoring of my service to the country. I really felt your pleasure, as I chatted with the President of the United States! A moment that I will never forget!

Mr. A, thanks to you I leave New York rejuvenated, inspired, and considerably healed. To quote the end of President Truman's Navy Day address:

> *"Indeed, the highest hope of the American people is that world cooperation for peace will soon reach such a state of perfection that atomic methods of destruction can be definitely and effectively outlawed forever.*
>
> *We have sought, and we will continue to seek, the attainment of that objective. We shall pursue that course with all the wisdom, patience, and*

determination that the God of Peace can bestow upon a people who are trying to follow in His path."

And that Mr. A, sums up my determination, as well!

Gratefully yours,

Max

On a train headed home to Salina!

Back Home

Tuesday, November 6, 1945

Dear Mr. A:

When I arrived in Salina last week, it seemed the entire town turned out to welcome me. It is beyond words to try to describe the warmheartedness and affection that has been shown towards me.

Apparently, the newspaper had gotten hold of a list of my war medals and the stories behind them, which they splashed on the front page. So now I am viewed as a war hero with which I am a bit uncomfortable. I mean, I don't feel like a hero.

To tell you the truth Mr. A, I feel incredibly disoriented, even in my own hometown. It is hard to describe. It is like I am a visitor or stranger, yet I know these people and this place. After all, I grew up here. Salina is still Salina. The townspeople are still the townspeople. But...

Even now, it seems that I am experiencing the colossal disruption more in Salina than New York City. It feels like all that was familiar has been leveled and hauled off, just as you described. On one hand, Salina remains the same town it always has been, and on the other hand, everything inside me has changed.

Part of me wants to flee to all that is familiar and wrap it around me like a comforting blanket, and pretend that I never experienced the war. Deep down I know that it is not only impossible, but it would cut short my healing by working through all the disruptions that I need to embrace.

Oh yes, then there are the nightmares, the flashbacks, waking up in cold sweats, and all the emotions lingering from the war just below the surface of my life.

I do want freedom. Freedom to live as the man I am intended to be. And, somehow I can sense there is no freedom in attempting to reconstruct my pre-war life. It is much clearer to me now that before leaving for OCS I was trapped in routines that I may have followed for the next 40 or 50 years, never finding my true self.

With the disruption of the war, I am realizing I have an opportunity to no longer be bound to everything which is not truest about me. Yet no one in Salina knows the new me, at least not yet. And that could pose another hurdle.

Already, the Grain Processing Company has graciously offered me a top management position. I guess they think that since I was an aide to a general, I may have more potential than being an assistant of the assistant to the assistant manager! (I'm chuckling as I write this. I still have my sense of humor, thank God!)

Ironically, this is the achievement of my 'dream' of a few years ago, 15 years ahead of my schedule! Do you remember when I wrote to you four years ago saying that it really isn't much of a dream, but more like a goal?

I do not want to be ungrateful to the grain company's very generous offer, but since my war disruption this feels like the old me in a better office with a larger paycheck and a fancy title. Oh, and did I mention the reserved parking space!?!

Four years ago, this would have been the crowning achievement of my life, yet today it seems hollow. Am I destined for more? Per your counsel, I am trying to "proceed slowly". There is great wisdom in your counsel to pace myself and receive healing until I have fully recovered my physical strength and emotional energy.

During my recuperation at your home on Long Island I learned that to pace myself requires discipline and honesty. Honesty to embrace the pain I have suffered, and discipline not to rush. In fact, I am recognizing that the emotional trauma I suffered is as real as any physical injury. And, it hurts. Some days I am fine, other days I am not. So, I just pause for however long I need. You were right when you wrote me in France, "you need as long as you need, no more and no less!"

While at war, there was never time to stop, we just kept pushing and driving to the next objective. And, subsequently we rolled up the enemy all the way to Berlin. By the way, that's *not* how General Patton would have described it, he used much more colorful language!

What you told me early on is now beginning to make more sense: that my pace will return as I heal, especially on the inside. Thanks to you and the doctors I have a better understanding of my suffering and the need for a complete healing. The counsel and wisdom you have given me is invaluable, not to mention your prayers of healing.

After experiencing such a colossal disruption of my life you asked me to consider:

"What path now?".

That simple question continues to reverberate in my head. At this point I'm not sure of the answer, and you suggested that could be the case.

Ever since I left France I have been sifting through my war journals and reflecting on my fellow soldiers' observations and reactions to me. Back home, I've found our past letters, especially those on dreams and desires and motives. Plus, I have been reviewing my original list of authentic characteristics in light of my Army experiences.

Curiously, I now seem to be clearer on what may be truest about me, even while disoriented and disrupted:

- I have big dreams.
- I am a warrior willing to fight.
- I am measured, but not hesitant.
- I can lead others and I am willing to take risks on the road to

victory and success.
- I am very relational.
- I am reliable, transparent, and plain spoken.
- I want to make a difference: help my fellow man and make this world a better place. (I was deeply stirred by the plight of the hungry and naked I saw during the war, especially in North Africa.)
- I love.

Mr. A, what are your reactions to what I am saying? Your opinions deeply matter to me. As I am immensely grateful for you coming alongside and guiding me over these last 4 years.

Again, thank you so much for welcoming me back home and helping me recover. I had no idea how exhausted I was or the toll taken on my spirit.

Thank you for providing medical treatment and covering the cost! It has made a huge difference. I feel much stronger and alert and physically pain free for the first time in over 2 years. Best of all were the hours you spent with me listening and comforting me. I will always remember your home as a place of healing.

Frankly, I am overwhelmed by your graciousness and generosity towards me. Your friendship means the world to me. I owe you so much, how can I ever repay you?

Love,

Max

Salina, Kansas (So glad to be home!)

What Path Now?

Monday, November 12, 1945

Dear Max:

As I read how you are orienting yourself to your disorientation, you actually had me with tears in my eyes and chuckling simultaneously. Continue your pursuit of healing and wholeness, and you will be stronger than you ever were. I am excited for you and the new adventure you are beginning.

Your characteristics list seems spot on to me, as it is reflecting your post-war maturation. Which leads me to pose this question: as generous as the grain company's job offer is, *does it fit the new man you are becoming?* I would not be too hasty in starting back to work until you settle that question.

Few men or women take the time to know who they truly are intended to be. But oh, what great rewards await those who choose to live into the freedom of their true self. You my friend have the rare opportunity to do more than heal, and that is a good thing!

You told me that you can live off your back pay for quite a while. Why not pursue the question: *"What path now?"*, a little longer? Perhaps you could look around the Salina area for hidden opportunities. Look for unseen potential or needs that only an entrepreneur can see.

Allow me to add that the jobs or work we do may simply be about earning a good living, and may not be the ultimate fulfillment of who we are, since that could occur elsewhere in our lives. However, there is the possibility there could be more, much more: living a fully integrated life as your true self.

Use your new perspective, Max. You have the potential, like Filippo Brunelleschi, to create and build domes into nothing but air! Or, as Thoreau described *"castles in the air"*.

Your disorientation provides an all new orientation.

And that my friend is the creative disruption you can now experience. That is the disruption that allows you to see what no one else can see.

You profoundly impress me Max North. You are a different man than you were 4 years ago. You have led men into battle, made life altering decisions, suffered hardships and defeats, and won great victories. It is no wonder that the grain company wants you in a top management position.

I affirm your decision to stay on the more difficult path of embracing the colossal disruption from your war experiences. Now begin to live into all the creativity that could flow from it. Be encouraged Max, for I can discern that you are being restored and coming alive in all new ways as a result.

For your strengthening,

Mr. A

New York City

P.S. And, Max, please discard the notion that you owe me anything. Whatever I may have contributed to you that is of value, I would ask that you pass it on to others for their benefit:

As I may have impacted you, so may you impact others.

A Sage Advice suggestion:

After completing *A Disruptive Reflection* on page 75, reconsider your truest characteristics list from page 56. Similar to Max deepening his characteristics list following his colossal disruption, so may you do the same. After reflecting on your disruption ask yourself, *"Now, what is truest about me?"*

A Crazy Hunch?

Friday, November 16, 1945

Dear Mr. A:

I must confess I don't believe I feel the same level excitement for my condition that you do, but perhaps I am being too serious. You mentioned that I am on a new adventure, which was not my perspective at all until pausing with your question: *"What path now?"*. Your advice to wait before accepting any job offers has helped free my imagination to all sorts of possibilities.

Mr. A, often I am hit with a sense urgency to rush an important decision. The urgency feels so real, like some kind of unseen, destructive force. Whenever I have pushed back against the urgency, deep down I can tell that I would have regretted the hurried decision. You are right that in this moment I should "not be too hasty". But this is quite hard for me to do, as it feels so counter-intuitive.

Almost every morning since I have been back in Salina, I take a run north of town through an old warehouse area out into the countryside. It has been a time of rejuvenation, free thought, and prayer. I have never paid much attention to the surroundings, as my focus was to get out to the open fields. That is until I read your letter.

Yesterday, as I was running back to town my gaze fixed on an old, rusting warehouse that has been an eyesore for years. I stopped and stared at it. I could literally feel my imagination coming alive visualizing all kinds of possibilities for that abandoned warehouse. Suddenly, a crazy idea began to emerge. Let me explain.

Before the war when I worked at the grain processing plant, I saw great inefficiencies and ways to make the distribution process of grain better. My hunch was that this could be applied to the entire food distribution network of the United States. Do you remember 4 years ago I told you that I had ideas to transform this industry? Well, this was what I was referring to.

Even as I write this, I recall in one of your first letters that you really did not have a great vision about the future of the telecommunications industry, but rather a hunch about the potential you saw. Maybe like you, this is my hunch! Or, is this just too crazy of a hunch?

My crazy hunch: Start a food distribution company and use this decrepit warehouse as the hub of operations. But there's more. What if this enterprise could be designed to also benefit those who truly suffer from hunger? Like those I came across in North Africa.

Since my return, I have felt at times that there are either no future possibilities for me, and then at other times I have felt that I have unlimited possibilities. Between my disruption and creativity it feels like I am riding an emotional roller coaster.

Yet, what is so freeing about my crazy hunch is that I do not sense any limitations, only unlimited possibilities. It seems that I may be turning a corner. Like a wind is blowing in my sails.

So, what do you think, Mr. A? Should I pursue it? Or, settle for something less crazy and more predictable?

Yours truly,

Max

Salina, Kansas

Trekking into the Unexplored

Wednesday, November 21, 1945

Dear Max:

Periodically on our life journey, we encounter a choice to continue down the path we know so well, or trek into new and unexplored territory. This is always followed by a second choice: to either trek in our own strength or with Divine Providence.

As you know, this is precisely the choice The Founders of our great nation faced in declaring independence from Great Britain. In essence, they decided to trek into the unexplored: *"...with a firm reliance on the protection of Divine Providence..."* (from the final sentence of the Declaration of Independence).

I am compelled to point out that this trek is a battle. It was a battle for The Founders to declare independence, a battle to gain independence, and a battle to stay independent.

Curiously, I have found that the more I rely on Divine Providence, the more I seem to be trekking into unexplored territory. And yes there are battles, some very hard battles. But I cannot imagine a richer and more fulfilling life, which I would never trade. In fact Max, I believe trekking with Providence is the highest adventure one can experience. That is why the final sentence from the Declaration of Independence is framed and hanging on the wall beside my office door.

And so, how should you decide? In all truth Max, this decision is yours, and yours alone. You mentioned that you sometimes pray when you run. Your 'running companion' to whom you pray is your best Helper, not me. Of course, I remain willing to share my experience with you, as much as you like. But, you are the one who lives the life resulting from your decisions.

Your questions: *"should I pursue this crazy hunch?"* or *"settle for the predictable?"* reveal you are in one of those life journey moments of choice. Based on my experiences, I can assure you that trekking into new and unexplored territory feels both crazy and about as certain as a hunch or as you described, an emotional roller coaster. However, pursuing the predictable is the well known path which may feel safer, but can ultimately be soul killing.

Max, in your letter of November 6th you will find embedded in your description of your true self, both identity and mission. Whether complete or incomplete I do not know, but your true self descriptors are connected to your deepest desires. *The truest things about you are your best guide to your best future.*

Trekking into the unexplored involves your possible callings in life, which may or may not have anything to do with how you earn money to live. Allow me to help sort this out.

~ Jobs, Careers or Crafts, Callings ~

Generally, a person's work can be categorized in one of three ways: jobs, careers or crafts, and callings. Each one is a bit more significant and unpredictable than the other.

Jobs are precisely that, jobs. It is work that pays the bills and keeps one financially afloat. Normally, the work is steady and predictable. Occasionally, a job may give clues about a future direction one may desire to pursue or not pursue. That is why I am a big believer that one should enjoy their work whenever possible.

A person's *career or craft* transcends jobs, and requires extensive training, education, and focus. A career does include jobs, but it is larger in purpose and mission. Most people think of their career or craft in terms of the rest of their working lives. Generally, there are twists and turns with ups and downs during one's career, often fluctuating with economic trends and cycles.

Callings transcend both careers and jobs, and may not even include them. They spring from the deepest and truest parts of who we are. By living into these true passions we will find greater fulfillment as the person we are intended to be. As we pursue our callings we may have little idea where we are headed and compensation often becomes irrelevant.

Callings run the gamut from the very broad, like fatherhood or motherhood, to the very unique and specific, such as your desire to feed the hungry in North Africa.

A curious secret I have discovered is that as we begin to step into our callings, we will begin to discover more of our authenticity and desires. And vice-versa: as we discover more of our authenticity, our callings become clearer. Max, these unexplored regions within us are vast and there is no map!

Notwithstanding, many miss their callings altogether, because they tend to hold the false belief that their job or career is one of the truest things about themselves.

~ Defining oneself ~

You might ask, how is this possible? Typically men define themselves by what they do, whereas women typically define themselves through their relationships. Thus, the basis of both genders' self-definition rely on false characteristics they may find in their work. Rarely does either gender begin with their truest characteristics. Thus, callings do not surface as a possibility.

Yet there is complexity, because in these mischaracterizations is some truth. Understand Max, oftentimes our job or career or craft will contain partial elements of who we are; so we settle for a little fulfillment falsely believing that is the best it can be.

Nonetheless, in our 'gut' we yearn for more. Deep down we somehow know more is actually possible. But we perceive there is a risk to discover it, and we are correct. Hence the choice of trekking into unexplored territories or remaining on our well known path.

Incidentally, it is never too late in life to trek into the unexplored or pursue calling. For I have known people who are advanced in years do precisely that, and have great impact.

How we live into our callings is as unique to us as our fingerprints, no two are alike; even the common callings like fatherhood or motherhood. So, Max, I would encourage you to vision each of the opportunities you have before you from the perspective of a job, a career, and even a calling.

In your imagination try on each opportunity like you would a jacket or a pair of trousers. See how they fit, walk around in them. Imagine your future self doing each of them. Consider these questions in this 'fitting room' of your mind:

- Do they fit who you truly are, the authentic you?
- How deeply are your desires stirred by each of them?
- How much do each of these tap into all your life experiences?
- Can you see yourself coming alive in these opportunities?

Now consider the desire you stated in your very first letter to me, hoping to become an entrepreneur. What is the state of that desire?

Look back on your achievements. Remember those times when you had more energy at the end of the day than at the beginning of the day. What you were doing? This is an incredibly helpful indicator, because those things that bring you more energy are sourced in your passions and point to the truest you.

As you assemble these clues to your true self and best future, listen to the sum of who you are: your body, soul, and spirit; heart, mind, and will. Listen to your 'running companion', too.

I await with great anticipation your findings and conclusions.

Your friend,

Mr. A

New York City

92

Getting off the Dime

Monday, November 26, 1945

Dear Mr. A:

Your most recent letter inspired me beyond words! Thank you so much. Even now, I am following your advice and have begun sorting through my opportunities in relation to jobs, careers and callings.

But first...!

I want to tell you what happened today, because my head is spinning with all sorts of ideas. In my last letter I described how each day I run past that abandoned warehouse.

After rereading your letter this morning, I decided to get off the dime and explore my dream by visiting that warehouse and see how I reacted. As I began nosing around it, I was startled by a voice behind me asking: *"Can I help you, son?"* It turns out the voice belonged to the caretaker who checks the property each week.

When I explained who I was and a little of what I was thinking, he was happy to show me around the entire site. He was just beginning his weekly property tour.

Mr. A, while it is still fresh I want to tell you what I experienced, even though it may sound a bit odd.

Initially what has excited me about this old warehouse is its location on the north side of town. On one side are rail lines, and on another side are truck bays facing a street that directly connects to the major highways U.S. 40 and U.S. 81. Plus, it is less than a mile by direct rail to the Grain Processing Company.

As I began to walk through the dilapidated place, something odd began to happen to me. It was as if this cavernous, empty warehouse came to life and was bustling with activity. Suddenly in my imagination, I was able to see racks to the ceiling filled with various containers of food, silos full of grain and corn. Men driving forklifts loaded with pallets. Shipments arriving in one set of doors, trucks and rail cars being loaded in another. There were even signs, *"To Africa: For the Hungriest"*, at several docks.

As I walked into the office, it too came to life. I could see it filled with desks, people answering phones, routing schedules on the walls, farmers being paid for their crops, agents selling grain to places all over the country.

Every part of the warehouse and surrounding property was bustling with activity.

I've never experienced anything quite like this. I do have a vivid imagination, but this was crazy! It appeared to be so real, so possible. Something deep inside me now seems to be saying, "This company will happen!" Have you ever experienced anything like this, Mr. A?

When I first read your last letter it seemed to be disconnected from the flow of our recent correspondence. Frankly, at first it did not make much sense to me. However, after this morning's tour of the old warehouse I am beginning to understand the point of your letter.

When I was the assistant of the assistant to the assistant manager that was just a job. It did give me a few ideas about me and my future, but it was just a job. The current job offer from the grain processing plant is really more of a career. It will put me on a track that could lead to President of the plant. I realize, that is something most people only dream about, but never realize.

Yet, seeing this warehouse come alive in my mind's eye... well, this feels more like destiny..., or do I daresay Divine Providence. It is as if the decision is deciding itself for me. So if my desire to help my fellow man in North Africa and elsewhere is actually a calling, then this potential food distribution company could be the way to make that calling a reality.

Mr. A, I am writing to you in the moment because I want to give you a sense of what I am experiencing. Four years ago when you first wrote me about your 'hunch', was it anything like this?

My enthusiasm and energy and passion is suddenly stirred to overflowing. To repeat myself, it feels like my mind is going in a thousand different directions of possibilities.

For instance...

This location is well-placed as a transportation hub for a food distribution company. Plus, it appears to have ample grain and food storage capacity; but it will require significant renovations in order to make it fully functional.

Furthermore, it seems to me that the distribution side of the grain company's business has been a headache to them for years. It is not their core business. However, I could make it my core business and solve their distribution problems by becoming the sole distributor of their product. In this way, I could launch a business with a large customer all at the same time.

Ok, I am getting way ahead of myself. My mind is going 100 mph surging with a multitude of ideas and possibilities!

Back to reality. The warehouse is in a state of considerable disrepair. Frankly everything about it appears depressing and hopeless. The caretaker told me that the city and county would like to tear it down, but can not afford to. They seized the property years ago due to back taxes.

What an amazing opportunity this could be for the town of Salina, if my vision became reality! This business would rehabilitate and make productive an old warehouse that is currently an eyesore. Over time, it could stimulate the economy of the area by bringing new jobs and more commerce. It could put Salina on the map!

Mr. A, can you get a sense of what I am imagining? Am I making any sense at all? I would love to know your reaction to all of this. Am I crazy? Is my hunch crazy?

There are so many details flying around in my brain. I've heard that the first to market has the greatest advantage. I do have a great rapport with the town and the grain company. I smell a fantastic opportunity, yet the obstacles seem insurmountable. But...

But, how do I start?

So Mr. A, I truly need your wisdom and experience in this moment, again! How would you suggest that I proceed? What do you see as my next step? Or, am I just thinking crazy?

However, beyond all that and most importantly in this week of Thanksgiving, I want you to know how thankful I am to you for all you have done for me, especially during my time of convalescence in New York. But even more than your gifts and actions, I am profoundly thankful for the relationship we enjoy.

Frankly, I could never write a letter like this or dream a dream like this or know the truest things about myself without you in my life. I am so deeply grateful to you Mr. A!

Happy Thanksgiving!

Max

Salina, Kansas

(sitting outside the old warehouse, my future business location???)

Pursuing a Hunch

Friday, November 30, 1945

Ah, Max...

Your letter arrived this morning and I simply had to respond, immediately. But first, let me wish you and your family a Happy Thanksgiving (a day late). Max, you are most welcome for any contribution I have made to you. It has been my pleasure.

In fact, I am most grateful to you for your boldness in writing that first letter to me four years ago. Your coming into my life has inspired and encouraged me in many different ways, which you may not even realize.

Now to your crazy hunch, the warehouse tour you described reminds me of memories from years long ago. I found myself consumed by your story. I read your letter so quickly, I have had to reread it to ensure I did not miss anything. The experience you describe has stirred something long forgotten in me and it is sweet! So thank you, my friend.

For you see Max, *the true mark of an entrepreneur is visioning opportunity where others do not.* The perceived opportunity is a reality to the entrepreneur, even though there is no visible evidence. The source for this visioning begins with the entrepreneur's true desires that flow from their true self, which can be particularly potent in conjunction with Providence. This is a foundational secret to entrepreneurial success.

Case in point, you can see a huge business opportunity in an old, abandoned warehouse. For entrepreneurs, this is an adventure into the unknown, and they love the whole idea of it! I always have. Do you? For others though, the warehouse is a problem to be solved, an eyesore to tear down.

Think back to the work you did prior to the war; identifying those characteristics that are most true about you. While in the Army you began living into those characteristics and became a more authentic man.

Over the years, I have discovered what is most true about a person sources from their dreams, desires, and even disappointments. The truest elements about a person begins before their earliest memories and points them towards their future direction. In other words Max, pursuing that which is most true about us can lead us into endeavors we never imagined.

In the Army, when you travelled cross country you would use a compass and shoot an azimuth based on true-north to keep you on course to reach your destination. Along the way, you would visually sight landmarks to remain on the right path of the azimuth. Connecting those landmarks one after another would ultimately bring you to your destination.

Your deepest desires, dreams, and passions are the equivalent of a personal true north, as they comprise who you are. Your desire to help your fellow man in North Africa is your destination. By connecting your authentic self to the vision for a food distribution company is plotting an azimuth that can give you the direction on how to reach your desired destination of feeding the hungriest.

So, who you are is point 'A' on the map. Helping your fellow man is point 'B" on the map. Your crazy hunch is how you will get from point 'A' to point 'B', i.e. your azimuth.

Another secret I have discovered is that the closer your destination lines up with your personal true north the more sustained passion you will bring to pursuing your crazy hunch, the azimuth. Which in truth, may not be so crazy after all.

Yes Max, my hunch was similar to yours, but different. As you may recall, I caught a vision for the burgeoning communications industry. It was not nearly as vivid as your vision, but I suspect just as exciting. Something deep inside me compelled me to follow this hunch. It was something I knew I had to do. Does this ring true for you?

There is so much more I would want you to know, but for now receive my encouragement: Pursue your hunch and see where it leads.

Fondly,

Mr. A

New York City

NOTES: How to Shoot an Azimuth...

An azimuth is a common military method to express direction. It is the direction of a compass bearing (the horizontal angle) measured in degrees in relation to true north. Using the compass to follow a precise compass bearing is called "shooting an azimuth."

To follow an azimuth as Mr. A describes, one simply does the following:

- *Identifies the points on a map where one is (point A) and where one wants to go (point B).*

- *To determine the azimuth, lay the compass on the map and line it up between point A and B on the map. Measure the number of degrees the line is from true north, for example 105 degrees. This is the azimuth.*

- *Now, physically stand at point A, point the compass directly in front of you and begin turning until the compass is 105 degrees from true north. This is "shooting an azimuth".*

- *Before walking in that direction, look for an object some distance away but in the line of direction the compass is pointing, for example a boulder.*

- *Upon reaching the boulder, recheck the heading to ensure you are facing 105 degrees, identify a new object and walk towards it.*

- *Continue repeating this process until you reach point B on the map which is the destination.*

The Decision

Tuesday, December 4, 1945

Dear Mr. A:

Thank you so much for sticking with me over these past 4 plus years. In 3 days it will be the date that *"…will live in infamy"*! So much has happened in my life, this country, and the world in only 4 years!

All your observations, insights, and counsel have been invaluable. Since my return to Salina, everything is happening so quickly and yet not fast enough. There is all the hoopla surrounding my return; lots of well wishers, job offers, parades, etc. All quite heady stuff. Then, there are the sleepless nights, the nightmares of war, and the yet to be resolved grief and losses.

You alone are a voice of calm, inspiring a measured response in an emotionally turbulent time for me. Trying to make clear headed decisions right now feels like I am trying to stand, unsupported on the deck of a boat which is being tossed about in 20 foot waves at sea. Much like some of the English Channel crossings I made.

Yet I know if I wait, the opportunity will pass me by. This is another carpe diem moment, similar to the time I accepted the offer to attend OCS without hesitation.

As a former tank commander, your azimuth illustration makes perfect sense. It does seem that my azimuth may point very closely in the direction of my personal true north. If I am to step out as an entrepreneur, I realize now is the time.

I have considered the alternatives of working for another man's vision or my own. Add to that my passion for the old warehouse, a food distribution company, and feeding the hungriest. All this adds up to something I really must try, even if I fail.

So, I have decided to pursue my hope and dream that I shared in my first letter to you:

I will pursue this entrepreneurial endeavor and go forward with the food distribution company idea.

Now, what do I do, Mr. A? (Just kidding! Knowing you well, I am certain you will not answer that question.)

Well, not really. What sage advice could you offer me now? If you can't tell, I am very excited!

Seriously, I do realize how the cumulative impact of your letters have prepared me for this moment. I do have a better sense of who I am and the vision I have for the future and the direction to go. Nevertheless, I need you in my life even more!

Love,

Max

Salina, Kansas

More to Know

Monday, December 10, 1945

Dear Max:

I share your observations of these past four years. Our worlds may never be the same, yet the future is bright. But Max, you are the one who is inspiring me! I remain humbled knowing the impact I have had on you. Thank you for including me in your journey.

I am thrilled with your clarity and decisiveness, even in the midst of disorientation and disruption. Max, your decision now sets things in motion. Allow me to elaborate a bit more from my last letter concerning *"...so much more I would want you to know...".*

How you pursue your hunch becomes all important. Pursue with wisdom, not haste. Pause, observe, listen, and reflect. Follow what is most true about who you are, and do not be diverted by the opinions of others.

Do not concern yourself with the greatness or size of the vision. Simply run after your vision with passion and authenticity.

By the way, great visions are rarely achieved in a lifetime, nor by a single person. It is only after said visions are realized can it be known whether they were truly great. Therefore, concern yourself with the pursuit and not its future impact.

I encourage you to journal all that you are experiencing. The very nature of journaling this vision will help you see it more clearly, while revealing important clues. You will be amazed at how often you will refer to this journal.

Max, *most only know their calling with certainty after they have begun living into it.* So, rather than puzzling over whether or not this vision is your calling; consider a more relevant question:

"What are you to now do with what has been revealed?"

It does appear that a journey is being laid out before you. A trek upon which you are willing to embark. So, consider your first step.

As you may suspect, the very nature of such a journey may include adventure, challenge, battle, victory, hardship, reward, etc. So, what can you know about it in advance? Its cost (which is much more than financial)? Its direction? What it may require of you?

Max, pause a moment, take a deep breath, relax. Step back from the present and observe your life. Realize that you are in an extraordinary moment of your life story.

Few men experience in a lifetime what you have experienced in the past four years. Having faced formidable challenges and horrors only found on the battlefield, you rose to the occasion and led men well. You have returned home a war hero and have been accorded a deep respect by many. It appears to me that you are in a singular moment of your life when a variety of opportunities and situations all converge in one glorious moment of opportunity.

Max, stand on that *"precipice"* overlooking a valley of opportunity below. You are already experiencing the excitement of it, while simultaneously finding it both exhilarating and scary. Yes, even a brave warrior like yourself may find himself hesitating at trekking into the unknown.

This is why, if you are centered on what is truest about you, your purpose, your identity; you will proceed in the right direction, especially if guided by Providence. A season like this is rare, and will not last. We can never stay on a precipice for very long. So, use this time wisely.

If you're so inclined, pray over it. Listen for that still, small voice inside you. What does your gut tell you? Apply any of these to assist you in discerning your first step.

Your friend,

Mr. A

New York City

Would You be Willing?

Friday, December 14, 1945

Dear Mr. A:

It was very helpful to pause and take multiple deep breaths! I was unnecessarily rushing due to a false sense of urgency, and your letter exposed that. Yet, you balanced the pausing with revealing this is a moment of opportunity that will not last forever. I understand.

So, I think it would be best for me to devote the next few months to organizing all my ideas into a plan before I begin to speak to others about it. My back pay from the Army will cover my expenses for quite a while, and the Grain Processing Company has generously allowed me plenty of time to make a decision on their job offer. So, I have the luxury of being able to think this through before I make any moves.

Nevertheless, it all feels urgent! I do seem to suffer from some sort of urgency malady, as I described in a previous letter. I can imagine you suggesting the antidote to urgency is doing the opposite. Which is precisely what you prescribed in your last letter!

So Mr. A, after taking another deep breath, I would like to ask you a straight up business question: Do you have any advice in regards to my inclination to organize all of my ideas for this business? Like how to put together some kind of guiding document? What do you think of business plans? I have heard a variety of opinions that range from positive to negative, even though I was thinking this might be a place to start.

Actually Mr. A, let me step back, "stand on the precipice", and ask you a more far-reaching question. Since you have been an invaluable sage in my life, I don't want to presume anything about our relationship. So my question is:

"Would you be willing to continue our correspondence and guide me as I pursue this entrepreneurial endeavor?"

For you have been exactly the kind of man I have so desperately needed to walk alongside me through my ups and downs. Our relationship means the world to me and I do not want anything to come between us, like business, which I know can be hard on friendships.

Yet, I can see I am now going to need business advice, too. Enlisting you as my entrepreneurial sage is my first step! Everything in me tells me to go to you first. So I am.

To be clear, what I said in my very first letter remains true. "...I am not looking for capitalization or contacts or anything like that." But, on the other hand I can't pay you for your business advice, even though I know that others may compensate you.

And do know Mr. A, I am 'ok' with any response you may have. Please let me know how you would like to proceed.

Gratefully yours,

Max

Salina, Kansas

P.S. Finally, Mr. A, I want you to know a principle of mine:

I will not seek your advice unless I intend to follow it.

In other words, if I have already decided a course of action, then I will not ask for your advice. I respect you, your wisdom, and your time way too much! So, if I am asking, then please know that your words carry great weight with me. Regardless, I will always tell you what I am doing and I always welcome your input.

PART THREE: The Secrets of an Entrepreneur

~ embarking into the world of business ~

Dear reader, that last letter from Max of December 14, 1945 was the final one in the original hidden cache of letters. Those of us who knew of these letters were left deeply perplexed, and not to say the least bit curious.

After all how would Mr. A respond to Max's invitation to advise him on his business endeavor? Would Max pursue his dream and start a new business or go back to his former employer? If he did launch his business idea, just how did Max do it? Oh, and just what was Mr. A's opinion of business plans?

Countless hours were spent searching Mr. A's papers and Mr. North's documents, but no letters were found. Nothing but silence seemed to be the answer from the past.

Until one day, while sitting at Mr. North's desk, an odd thought occurred to me to look in the place where the original hidden cache of letters were discovered. And this truly is another story for another time, but suffice it to say that I found another hidden place inside the hidden place, and inside it was a carefully sealed parcel with this note on the outside:

The Secrets of an

Entrepreneur

~ M. North

I carefully unwrapped the parcel. It contained more letters! Immediately, I saw the date of the first letter on top: December 20, 1945 and it was from Mr. A. Certainly, this was the next letter in the correspondence chronology!

But why would Mr. North separate these letters from the others?

The first letter gives a clue. In it Mr. A alters the direction of their correspondence and relationship. In fact, there are two parts to this letter: the first part appears to bring some closure to their past correspondence, and the second part introduces Max to business secrets that Mr. A regularly used.

As I read these letters, a question dawned on me: "Had Mr. A been preparing Max for this letter from the beginning of their relationship?" I have since discovered in a journal of Mr. A's he considered sharing his business ideas with Max a possibility, because of Max's first letter about his entrepreneurial hopes.

Mr. A journaled his amazement of Max's receptivity to his guidance and his diligence in answering his questions. Through their various encounters and letters he had become quite fond of Max, almost like a son.

Apparently, Max had reiterated several times to Mr. A (as he did in his first letter) that he sought no money or favors or any kind of resources from him, other than his wisdom and advice. Clearly, Mr. A could have provided Max great advantages, but he respected Max's wishes and submitted.

According to his journal, Mr. A realized that Max had to discover for himself that he had *"what it takes"* to be an entrepreneur, as per his letter of January 14, 1942. Much like Mr. A had discovered some 40 years earlier in his own life.

Truly, we had stumbled upon the most precious letters of their correspondence. What Max had labeled:

The Secrets of an Entrepreneur.

Contained in these letters were answers to all of our questions and so much more. Best of all, Mr. A's greatest secret was included: how to *map your direction.*

And, mapping your direction is absolutely critical if you ever intend to *build a great company*!

NOTES: On Sage Advice Applications...

In Parts One and Two "Sage Advice to Apply" pages were included to help you apply the advice and applications that Mr. A was giving to Max.

In Part Three there is no "Sage Advice to Apply" because Mr. A provides detailed explanations guiding Max in all the steps to develop The Next Level Navigator for his entrepreneurial "hunch".

Likewise dear reader, you can develop The Next Level Navigator for your

- *Ongoing, well-established company, or*
- *Business startup or new company, or*
- *Personal Next Level.*

Simply follow Mr. A's instructions to Max and develop your Navigator, as Max develops his. All of Max's responses are included, providing you with excellent examples of how each step could be done.

To go further, explore www.LiveTrulyFree.com.

A Shift in the Relationship

Thursday, December 20, 1945

Merry Christmas, my dear Max!

Thank you for telling me about the difference I have made in your life. We can live a lifetime and never know the impact we may have had in the life of another. So, I am blessed by your words.

There is much to respond to in your letter. I will begin by saying that few have the wisdom that lies behind your insight recognizing how mixing business with a personal relationship may endanger a friendship. Our friendship is precious to me, on this point we are in agreement that it must always come first.

I am stirred with excitement for you and this grand adventure on which you have decided to embark. I will gladly provide whatever guidance I can. You are wise to think through the journey before you begin.

Max, let me try to describe where I imagine you are today and where you may be in the near future. From your previous letter I gather that you recall what you wrote to me in the fall of 1941?

You described the feeling of being brought to the edge of a precipice and looking out on a new vista of endless possibilities, yet also being able to look back on old paths of familiarity. Then the war completely disrupted that moment.

Now you are back in Kansas, but you are changed. Wiser with experience, yet significantly shaped by the war. Colossal disruptions do that. One can choose to be hardened by the experience or tenderized by it.

Instinctively, people often choose to be hardened as a way to self-protect themselves from further suffering. And yes Max, it is a choice. But, it also prevents them from experiencing the deeper joys. To be tenderized by suffering means to embrace the pain of the moment, forgive and move on. Essentially, one will miss a rich and abundant life, if they choose to be hardened.

Max, I sense that you are now back on that precipice of a mountain overlooking a great valley. The air is clearer and fresher, and you can see the lay of the land much better. There are great stretches of green that are trees, large boulders appear as only small pebbles in the distance. Huge waterfalls are simply thin white lines. You see the beauty and grandeur of this place. But due to the distance, there is much you do not see.

Now, you have chosen to descend into this valley and soon you will be navigating through a variety of challenges. Consequently, you will lose sight of the view you have today. Rarely, can one have both the mountain view and the valley view, simultaneously.

This is why I am encouraging you to write down what you are envisioning in great detail. For it will fade over time, even to the point you cannot remember it at all. You will need this detailed description of your vision when you find yourself overwhelmed by the obstacles, distractions and minutia of the valley. And trust me, it will happen.

So, as you journal every detail of what you are seeing, do not be concerned about organizing your thoughts. Just capture them for now. *I have discovered that the simple act of writing one's ideas sharpens the brain's ability to recall and deepen those ideas, later.*

~ ~ ~ ~ ~ ~ ~ ~

Max, in all of our correspondence I have offered you very little clear-cut, practical business concepts or advice. For to have done so would have distracted you from the deeper questions of life upon which we have engaged.

I have lived a lot of life, had failures, ruined close relationships before I realized this secret:

Discover what is most authentic about you,

111

experience healing from your disappointments, and
live into your true self: the person you are intended to be.

If you begin there, all your endeavors will become much clearer. And, remember King Solomon's counsel: *"Above all else guard your heart* (the sum of all you truly are), *for it is the well-spring of life* (it determines the course of your life)".

Years ago in my telegraph days I read this quote as it came over the wires from a speech President Theodore Roosevelt gave in France. It fully propelled me into the world of entrepreneurism.

> *"It is not the critic who counts, not the man who points*
> *out how the strong man stumbled, or where the doer of*
> *deeds could have done better. The credit belongs to the*
> *man who is actually in the arena, whose face is marred*
> *by dust and sweat and blood, who strives valiantly, who*
> *errs and comes short again and again, who knows the*
> *great enthusiasms, the great devotions, and spends*
> *himself in a worthy cause, who at best knows*
> *achievement and who at the worst if he fails at least*
> *fails while daring greatly so that his place shall never*
> *be with those cold and timid souls who know neither*
> *victory nor defeat."*

"The arena" that one may enter can take many forms, and you my friend are no *"cold and timid soul"*! For you have already experienced achievement in one such *"arena"*, *"while spending yourself in a worthy cause"*, World War II.

Now you are choosing to enter the arena again, but in a different configuration! The flow of your life along with your intentionality has brought you to this place of pursuing your dreams and entering the arena of entrepreneurism.

Max, when this arena is viewed from "the precipice" it may appear as the source of fulfillment of all ones dreams. However, as you descend down into the valley, otherwise known as *"the arena"*, that is when one's *"face is marred by dust and sweat and blood"*.

I have found the arena of entrepreneurism to be a constant source of *"new and unexplored territory"*. Do you recall what I wrote about the battles when you choose this path?

"And yes there are battles, some very hard battles. But I cannot imagine a richer and more fulfilling life, which I would never trade."

It has been in the crucible of this arena that Providence has refined me and taught me these secrets that I now share with you. Life does not become easier, nor necessarily harder, as an entrepreneur. But, as I have embraced the battles, and yes the pain too; I have grown in love, humility and wisdom; all essential ingredients to being truly successful in this life.

To that end, let me share a practical business thought or two.

As to your question concerning business plans, I suggest you wait. A business plan is a great discipline to help you and any partners think through all the details of your endeavor, but it is no guarantor of success. The best assurance of success is the intense look in the eye of the entrepreneur and the fire in his belly to succeed, no matter what. So how does one acquire that?

Max, your instincts serve you well. Trust them, as the best place to begin. You need to harness your passion and your intensity into that "guiding document" you have suggested. As you do, your business endeavor will become very real to you and then to all with whom you share it. So much so, that others may be persuaded to join you in your endeavor.

The secret is to strike a balance between the detail of a business plan and the lack of preparedness in simply pursuing a passion. In other words, it is best to avoid over-thinking the endeavor, but at the same time not to under think it, as well.

Years ago, I developed a one-page document that aligned me, my leadership team and the entire company in a new direction to achieve a new level in a new way. My company had stagnated, badly. We had lost our momentum and desperately needed a breakthrough to a Next Level.

Today, that one-page document is our single most, powerful strategic guide. It goes well beyond the generalities of vision and mission statements, yet avoids the minutia of a business plan. It is a living document that we use regularly to direct us. I call it:

The Next Level Navigator.

The Navigator may be just the right strategic process you are needing to help organize your passions and ideas into launching your business endeavor.

Not only does it work well in helping existing companies breakthrough to their Next Level, but it has worked well for enterprises that are new or forming. In fact, I have seen it work for almost any kind of endeavor. It even helps individuals achieve their personal Next Levels. In your situation Max, your company's Next Level will be its First Level.

How does The Next Level Navigator sound to you? Might it be something you would be interested in developing for your venture?

If this idea appeals to you, I would be willing to guide you through a series of questions over a course of letters that would develop all the elements required to create it.

Regardless of how you desire to proceed Max, my answer is a resounding 'yes' to your request that we continue our correspondence as you pursue any entrepreneurial endeavor.

All in with you,

Mr. A

New York City

Yes, Yes, Yes!

Thursday, December 27, 1945

Merry Christmas to you, Mr. A! (2 days late)

I have lost count how many times I have read your last letter since I received it. I have so many thoughts swirling in my head, but first let me say Mr. A, you are both a sage in my life and my friend.

Yes, yes, yes! I absolutely desire your assistance, guidance and wisdom. I am so humbled, thrilled, and truly blessed by your willingness to come alongside me in this way!

The precipice, the valley, the arena are all great metaphors that are helping me locate where I am in this moment. The Roosevelt quote is one I shall never forget. I had never thought of my war experiences as being in "the arena", but it makes complete sense.

In the war my troops and I experienced setbacks and defeats, but we kept fighting for breakthroughs and continued advancing to victory. Although I experienced horrific losses, most deeply some close friends whom I shall never forget; I also experienced great victories and participated in setting many people free from the oppression of tyranny!

Thanks for showing me how entrepreneurism is another way to participate in "the arena". The stakes are not life and death, as in war; but the stakes are still high, as one could lose their livelihood and financial security. There is much risk. There are winners and losers. But, there is also the possibility of freedom! Freedom to pursue one's own vision and passion, all the while living into one's true self!

As you advised me, I am journaling all of my thoughts and ideas about my business idea, the future company, the old building, the processes, the employees as a team, etc. I even have a whole section in my journal called *Envision*.

Even still Mr. A, my ideas feel far-fetched. Or perhaps more accurately, my ideas feel assaulted. Do you remember writing me about "gathering storm clouds" shortly before the attack on Pearl Harbor?

I responded that it never occurred to me that evil could be directed at me. After 4 years of war, not only do I know that can be true, but I know what it feels like to have the enemy searching to destroy me (and my troops). This current assault feeling is similar.

I think that is why I was asking you about business plans. I have been trying to develop some financial projections, like those found in business plans, to determine how this venture might succeed financially. In all honesty, I am looking for some kind of assurance that I can succeed at this venture.

But as you recently wrote me, *"to trek into new and unexplored territory... is always followed by a second choice: to either trek in our own strength or with Divine Providence."*

I believe Providence may be more in my envisioning, and I may be operating more in my own strength by doing projections. Perhaps, I am trying to turn "new and unexplored" into a sure thing. In truth, my numbers are sourced more from my imagination than reality. So, why not trek with Providence!?!

So, yes! I desperately need your guidance, and would love to develop The Next Level Navigator with you. As you may have guessed, I am running in circles and don't have a clear picture of where I am headed or where to start.

So, how do I start, Mr. A? As, I really do want to launch the business as soon as possible. Ready to go...

Happy New Year!

Max

Salina, Kansas

Ready, FIRE, Aim

Wednesday, January 2, 1946

Dear Max:

Happy New Year! May it be full of great blessings for you. How appropriate to begin this process at the beginning of a new year, although we could begin it at any time.

I love your enthusiasm and energy with such transparency! Your honesty has accurately captured your dilemma. As human beings we want both the thrill of adventure and the security of a sure thing. You conclude well my friend, to not trek in your own strength.

Furthermore, I can assure you that financial projections serve no purpose unless you first know precisely where you are headed. I have yet to meet an entrepreneur who was not ready to start their business the instant they were struck by the proposition of their vision.

In fact, many entrepreneurs operate with a "ready, *FIRE,* aim" approach! Sometimes they hit the mark, but typically they miss more than they hit. Their solution? Shoot more. Thereby increasing their odds that they will have a few hits. In business, as in the military, misses can be expensive, especially for a new company. It can ill afford many missteps, since it has no previous hits, i.e. successes, to absorb any setbacks. Suffice it to say that I know this approach all to well. Some may say that I even invented it!

After years of having many more misses than hits I developed a new approach:

"ready, aim, FIRE"!

A revolutionary concept, is it not my dear Max!?! My process will slow you down a bit on the front end, but I believe you will avoid costly pitfalls and stumbles as you launch your company. Plus, you may find yourself further ahead, sooner rather than later.

The idea of The Next Level Navigator is to *shoot less and hit more*. Oh, I still miss the mark at times, but I assure you that I have many more hits than misses. This gives me the distinct advantage of not having to expend all the energy and resources involved in wasted shots, which I call *avoidable failures*.

The Navigator is a versatile document with an adaptable process. It has been used to help steer my company through many stages of development and many economic times from its first breakthrough to the present day.

We have applied it to departments within our company, the suitability of potential mergers and acquisitions, and possible company spinoffs. At times the Navigator has helped us in raising funds from banks or investors, and even recruit key employees. Furthermore, The Navigator serves as a great agenda to guide the strategy meetings of our leadership team.

Max, as a point of interest, I would reiterate that individuals at our company have also used The Navigator to ascertain their own personal Next Level, including myself.

The bottomline is that this process is designed to keep pace with a constantly developing company and ever-changing business environment. In fact, my leadership team periodically revisits the process to keep The Navigator relevant for our company. Hopefully, you will see its many possibilities and applications.

The Next Level Navigator works because it is anchored in story, beginning with yours! Every ongoing entity carries the imprint of its founders and current leaders, whether they realize it or not. When this process is used with an ongoing company, it relies on the history of the company while considering the impact of its key leaders' story upon it. When it is used for a new company or a fresh business venture idea, it focuses on the personal history of the founding entrepreneur(s).

Trust me in this Max, for if your company succeeds your imprint on it will be huge. That is why knowing who you are and your story is so important for your company to begin well. Therefore, why not be intentional with that imprinting?

Thus, all your previous work matters to The Navigator process. Knowing what is most authentic about you, the processing of your desires and disappointments, and your journaling about your business idea will all be used. We will pour all of that into The Navigator because:

the sum of who you are will be
the heart and soul of your company.

Never forget this secret Max, as this is true for any company and its founders.

As I wrote in my previous letter, I will "guide you through a series of questions over a course of letters". Your answers will develop different parts of The Next Level Navigator for your business venture. At the end of the process we will pull all your answers together into a single page document.

Now hear this tip-off: *do not over-think your answers to these questions*! Simply apply your best creativity to each question in the moment. Typically, your first, instinctive response may be the best. The process is designed to keep evolving and refining your answers, so your first answers will not be your final answers.

Enclosed is a separate document I wrote that details the essence of the process and begins the first step. I look forward to hearing your response!

Fondly,

Mr. A

New York City

~ The Essence of *The Next Level Navigator* ~

This is the document that Mr. A enclosed with his letter of
Wednesday, January 2, 1946.

Max, as you begin The Next Level Navigator allow me to provide some contextual understanding to the process. Actually, I would love to tell you the whole story of how The Navigator came about, but I will reserve that for another letter.

Several years after beginning my company I inadvertently discovered we were running into what felt like invisible barriers to growth, which I would eventually refer to as Success Barriers. Ironically, it was not until a prospective buyer of the company observed that our growth seemed restrained, that I realized something was wrong. In truth, we were in a slow decline but I had not perceived it, as I was busy working 60 to 80 hours a week!

Looking back, I now realize that I could no longer get around all the elements of the company. A transformation was required if we were to break through our Success Barriers and reach our Next Level. Most startling and freeing was discovering that *change had to begin with me*, the founding entrepreneur. If I could modify my modus operandi (entrenched way of operating), then that could release everyone else to change theirs.

Thus, The Navigator process was born out of our huge need for fundamental change and a way to do it! Enclosed is more of my primitive artwork to help you visualize this story that leads a company to its Next Level.

Success Barriers

To begin this process one has to identify Success Barriers that may be holding them back. These barriers can look very different

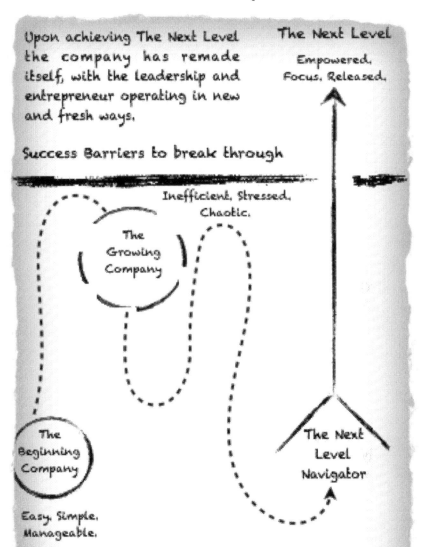

Upon achieving The Next Level the company has remade itself, with the leadership and entrepreneur operating in new and fresh ways.

Success Barriers to break through

The Next Level

Empowered. Focus. Released.

Inefficient. Stressed. Chaotic.

The Growing Company

The Beginning Company

Easy. Simple. Manageable.

The Next Level Navigator

The line of the circle represents the entrepreneur/owner trying to get around all the elements of the company. As the company bumps into Success Barriers, cracks appear in the circle line reflecting the inability of the entrepreneur/owner to keep up. A transformation is needed in order to grow!

from one company to another, but they all have the same net effect: *a company's forward progress stalls.*

For example, if a company is trying to add employees they may add 2, but later lose 3; or expand into a new territory, but lose traction in an existing one; or sales grow beautifully in a new revenue stream, but other revenue streams begin to slip.

Sometimes the barriers can be internal to the entrepreneur, similar to my experience of working 60 to 80 hours a week and falling further and further behind. Or, one day the entrepreneur looks up and has no family life or outside relationships. Or, they are just simply exhausted.

The possible evidences of barriers are endless. Sadly, many companies and entrepreneurs may struggle for years never realizing Success Barriers and the need for transformation.

For a new company just forming they have Success Barriers, too. In fact many would argue these are the toughest ones to overcome, because the company has no momentum, no progress, or no track record of success upon which to build. Thus begins *the* battle to trek into the unexplored, and oh the sweetness that occurs as one begins to triumph over these barriers!

More Insights into Next Levels

I have found that the best way for one to overcome Success Barriers is for the company to have a clear and compelling Next Level to move towards.

The Next Level Navigator is an intentional choice to change the way a company and its leaders operate at every level in order to reach new heights, because the old methods are no longer effective. For a new company these methods would be the initial ways it would operate to reach its First Next Level.

Max, for a company to determine its Next Level it must know in which direction it is headed. It is like standing on *that* precipice seeing the horizon many miles away. What does the entrepreneur envision for their new business undertaking? Or, what does the entrepreneur and core team envision next for their ongoing enterprise? This is so very important in the determination of Next Levels.

Interestingly, I have discovered many companies have never truly envisioned their distant futures. Instead, they often substitute financial objectives for where they are headed. I contend that *great financial results are byproducts* of envisioning and achieving Next Levels, not the purpose.

My experience suggests a company's initial envisioning of their future may convey the basic idea, but it is a more of a placeholder. It takes time and movement towards Next Levels for envisioning to become clearer. Ultimately, a true vision is huge and will take years to accomplish, maybe more than a lifetime. That is why that vision is on the distant horizon.

I have enclosed another of my 'beautiful illustrations':

The Next Level is much closer than the horizon. It is comparable to being over a hill. *The path to achieving it can not be known, yet you can know what it is.* Reaching The Next Level is always moving a company towards its vision. Time-wise, The Next Level is 3 to 5 years away.

So, what do we call what we *can see* to achieve? The Next Strategic Step, because the route to it can be known and usually requires 6 to 12 months. As one Next Step is achieved, the next one emerges until eventually The Next Level is reached.

The Quintessence of The Next Level Navigator

The Next Level Navigator process is disruptive by design. If done well, the process will shake up status quo thinking. I know it does that for me.

It is simple in concept, and powerful in results! Its foundational premise assumes companies are willing to build on their strengths while abandoning their weaknesses, a tall order for many.

The transformation begins with the people. All the essential people in my company know our Next Level and strategies. In fact every person in the company, to one degree or another, helps accomplish parts of the Next Step strategies required to reach the company's Next Level.

The Navigator demands adaptability and responsiveness. My leadership team and I have developed a habit of using our Next Level Navigator to stay on course, remember our strategies, and monitor our progress. It guides us in shifting responsibilities, shedding status quo, and stepping into expanded roles. In fact, all major business decisions are made contextually with our Navigator.

I have found that companies using The Navigator can remain nimble and responsive in ever-changing, competitive markets without losing focus on their chief aim: achieving their Next Level.

We stay agile by conducting periodic reviews of The Next Step strategies which continually verify the relevance of our Next Level.

These reviews are especially crucial for companies just starting out. Typically, new companies will make several significant pivots towards their First Next Level, often requiring updates to their initial Navigator.

It is almost as if The Navigator will not allow itself to become static and unresponsive, like a business plan left in some executive's desk drawer.

How to Begin The Navigator Process

So Max, we will begin The Next Level Navigator process by envisioning your company's future. To do this, let us go back to your dreams.

Do the following:

Simply write your dreams in whatever format flows freely for you: paragraphs or sentences or lists. Do not refer to any previous writings. Do not worry about the size or craziness of your dreams. Simply, write a free flow of thought for 30 to 45 minutes in a quiet and uninterrupted place.

Let your dream writing include both your personal and business venture dreams. Start with a blank page and simply write your dreams from the truest part of you.

Finally, do not critique or edit your dreams, that will occur later. When you are finished set your papers aside and let it rest.

From the Journal of Mr. A

NOTES: Additional Navigator Insights...

In reviewing other materials and notes of Mr. A's, a few more insights into The Next Level Navigator process were found.

- *It is an iterative process, meaning that each time you rewrite your answers you will improve them. So, repetition is the key to success. If it feels like the same answer may apply to several questions, it is best to write fresh answers to each question. In other words, do not simply copy previous answers.*

- *Mr. A understood how our minds refine and improve ideas through rewriting. However, he also knew that at some point rewriting can become overkill. His guidance to Max was to guard against overthinking his replies. Recognize when that is happening, and move on to the next item.*

- *In one of Mr. A's notes he compared developing and expressing ideas like that of sighting in a rifle. One takes a shot, sees where it hits, adjusts the gunsight, takes another shot, so on and so forth until every shot hits the bullseye. The same holds true for finding the best words for ideas in The Navigator. With practice you will know when you are hitting the bullseye with your strategic phrasings.*

- *The Next Level Navigator develops precision in expressing strategy, it also helps companies hit moving targets with precision. Mr. A knew that the more precisely worded the strategy, the greater the odds of achieving it.*

NOTES: For Ongoing Companies...

In letters written several years later, Mr. A would take Max through the entire process again because The Food Transport Co. had achieved its First Next Level.

He had Max do a quick review of his envision statement, guiding principles, company strengths and promise to establish where the company was at that present time. But, then had him jump straight into The Next Level process.

We would suggest the same for the reader who has an ongoing company. Read those letters to ensure you have clearly expressed all the core strengths about where your company is today. Improve any of them that need improving, then begin the process with the letter titled: *The Next Level.*

We feel certain that Mr. A would agree that there is no point in repeating work you have already done well!

Dreams to Envisioning

Thursday, January 3, 1946

Dear Max:

It occurred to me after I had already posted yesterday's letter that I should give you a few more details to enhance the dream list assignment.

Once you have written your dreams, I would like you to take a different approach to your vision of the business to lay the groundwork for what I call an Envision Statement. This is a brief statement that clearly illustrates what you envision this company becoming many years from now.

To begin writing this statement I would like you to imagine your business venture 20, 30, or even 50 years from now. Using your imagination, employ all five senses. Describe your experience by writing everything down. What do you see, hear, feel, smell, and even taste?

There could be numerous approaches to imagining your business. A simple possibility would be to imagine a walk-through of all the areas and aspects of your company, whether you have one location or many locations.

Below are a list of questions to prompt your imaginary company walk-through. As you follow your imagination, more details and observations will occur to you far beyond this list:

- As you arrive at the company, what do you experience?
- What is happening at the company?
- How would you describe the various areas / locations of the company, as you walk-through?
- What are the processes / work flows like?
- How would you describe the culture of the organization?
- What sort of camaraderie exists?

- Describe the employees, as you encounter them.
- What is the experience of customers or users as they engage the company and use its products or services?
- What do vendors experience as they encounter the company?
- What do you observe as the strengths of the business?
- What are areas that need improvement?
- Overall, what sort of feeling do you get?
- What are the hallmarks of the company?
- What else?

Max, by writing out your dreams and envisioning your company you are well on your way to completing The Next Level Navigator. Let me know when you are done and I will send you the next step.

Warmest regards,

Mr. A

New York City

NOTES: How to Imagine 'Virtual' Locations...

In today's world, more and more companies are virtual or have virtual locations or have employees working virtually, anywhere in the world. In other words, there may be no physical location to imagine.

For these companies, this exercise can be even more powerful because through imagination it forces assimilation of the company into an actual company.

Simply imagine the company in a singular space. Imagine its culture, communications, interactions, work flows, etc. as if it is not separated by miles. Then, imagine how to bridge those gaps of miles, so that it feels and operates as a singular space company. Then, compare the two imagining lists and refine into one list.

Ready...

Monday, January 7, 1946

Dear Mr. A:

Before I read your letter of January 2nd I definitely felt that I knew my target and I was ready to start "firing", like any other well intentioned entrepreneur! After all, what could be clearer than my ambition to go ahead with a grain transportation company!?!

When I first read your letter I assumed that most entrepreneurs would know their target, like I knew mine. It's simple, right? We have the idea of the business we want to launch, so we go do it. Mr. A, I think you may be saying *that would be the "firing" without "aiming", much less being "ready"*.

Now I am realizing that what I think is my target is like saying the shooting range is my target. It's not. The target is somewhere at the shooting range. I need to find and focus on my specific target and that is what you must mean by *"aiming"*.

My analogy may not be the best Mr. A, but I am trying to express how I thought I knew my target and was "aimed". However, you have already exposed that I would have just been shooting in the general direction of my target and hoping to hit something. In fact if I did hit something, I could have mistakenly concluded that was my target, since I hit it.

How ironic! That is exactly the opposite of how I commanded in the Tank Corps. We could only carry so many rounds in a tank, so we had to be selective and intentional in choosing only those targets that would help us achieve our mission. We never shot hoping to hit something. So, why would I start doing that now?

Recognizing that most entrepreneurs have a limited number of 'shots' like money, energy, and other resources; why would they still use a 'hit or miss' or 'trial and error' approach? After all, it's only after not hitting anything with their 'shots' that they begin to determine what their real target is. By that time they could have run out of 'ammo'. I now see how too many misses could mean the end of pursuing one's endeavor before ever beginning.

Thus, I have followed your advice, and I did not refer to my previous journaling, instead I commenced fresh. What I have written is clearer, more succinct and powerful than anything previous. I am surprised that even some of my dreams as a boy remain very real.

For example, even though I grew up in the Midwest I wanted to be a cowboy, and that desire for adventure remains very real in my dreams. I can see how riding on the open range could connect to my entrepreneurial desire by being free of following anyone else's vision.

I hope all this makes sense. After completing my dream list and my company "walk-through" I am still bursting with more ideas due to your questions, so I keep journaling them. I feel like a kid again, dreaming and imagining. It is so fun. My joy is returning! Somehow I suspect you knew that could happen.

So Mr. A, without your guidance I would be like other entrepreneurs: "aiming" after I would have 'shot and missed', maybe even using all my 'ammo'! Thank you so much for explaining your approach: *aiming first. It's so obviously brilliant, few probably ever do it!*

I've included a carbon copy of my dreams and envisioning assignment. *So, Mr. A what's next?* When can I start *"firing"*?

Now!?!

Max

Salina, Kansas

~ *Max's Dream List and Envision Application* ~

Dream Lists:

- *to pursue my vision, not someone else's*

- *to risk, face challenges, find rewards of an entrepreneur*

- *revolutionize the food distribution systems of America*

- *alleviate some hunger in the world, and other suffering, too*

- *deliver food and clothing to the hungriest in the world beginning in Africa*

- *I still want to be a cowboy riding the open range not knowing what each day will bring, except more adventure*

- *be an explorer*

- *establish a profitable food transport company that diverts part of its success / profits to benefit the hungriest*

- *to be married to a woman with whom we can share each other's dreams and passions - to be a great husband*

- *to have children who flourish - to be a great father*

- *travel the world to really learn about other cultures and places*

- *to live a life that benefits others*

- *to not do business alone, instead build a great team of people of similar passions*

- *to create / innovate new methods in the food industry that transform it forever*

- *to make a positive impact on the world*

The Envision Application:

- *it is a friendly and relaxed atmosphere*

- *everyone knows their role and is invested in doing a good job*

- *the company is innovative, efficient and evolving*

- *it is constantly focused on how to do it better, easier, faster for the benefit of the end customer*

- *the company is relational - it is all about people helping people whether it is a customer or vendor or employee*

- *we have fun together as a company*

- *devise some sort of formula that for every mile of delivered goods driven or pounds delivered, a hungry person is fed a meal*

- *involve customers and vendors and employees in this goal to alleviate a little suffering*

- *great growth and profits to expand and be the premier food transportation company in the midwest and eventually the U.S.*

- *partner with our customers to deliver the freshest and healthiest products to the kitchen table*

- *ultimately provide all transportation involved from the field to the kitchen table*

- *reliable, fast, friendly service*

- *don't squeeze every nickel out of every deal with vendors or customers, profits are important but so are our relationships with others*

The Secret to the Process

Friday, January 11, 1946

Dear Max:

Your authenticity and passion serve you well. However, tuning your ear to wisdom will serve you even better.

Early on in my life I did act prematurely by "firing" first without "aiming". My impetuousness created almost insurmountable obstacles. Your observation that many fire and miss in search of their target is spot on. Thus, your willingness to pause and follow this process is a testament to your character and wisdom.

Max, the truest parts of us, our true selves, are like natural springs bubbling with fresh ideas. Capture those ideas by writing them down. I find that the more I write, even more ideas will flow.

At this early stage it is good to have too many ideas, instead of not enough. And please treat every idea as a good idea. Ultimately, we will narrow all those ideas to the best ones. Some ideas may be used later, others maybe never at all, but for now consider them all good.

Now, I would like to share with you the secret to success with this process: it is the technique of writing and rewriting. Every time I restated an idea *(not copied, but rewrote)*, I discovered that it became stronger with more clarity through preciseness.

So, I trained myself not to recopy ideas verbatim, but to actually restate them, often triggering more ideas. As you will experience, The Next Level Navigator involves writing and rewriting. And that my friend is *the secret to the process.*

So, Max, I would like you to apply the following to both your dream list and your envision application.

- Carefully reread what you have written. Identify key elements contained in your writings. Look for patterns and groupings.

- Now list and group the key elements, as best you can. Remember to rewrite these elements, not copy them.
- Circle the top ten elements that most clearly relate to your business venture.

The results will be 2 lists (one for dreams and one for envision) of 10 elements each. Now, select and rewrite the best ten elements from the 2 lists. Once your list is complete, rank each of the 10 elements by placing a number from 1 to 10 by each one.

Max, this final list of the best ten elements is what you envision your company becoming. However, there is one more distillation needed: *write an envision sentence.*

The idea is to craft these elements into a single sentence that completely describes what you envision this company becoming. Start with a paragraph of words and keep skimming it down until it is a sentence. The key is for the sentence to be easily understood and remembered. Plus as the name implies, it creates a picture!

At this point I would encourage you to heed the words of Polonius from William Shakespeare's play, Hamlet:

"Brevity is the soul of wit."

That is to say, make each word convey significant meaning. Practice the rewriting process, and allow your mind to precisely seek the exact words that capture the essence of your visioning for your enterprise. One clue I could offer is that the top three to five elements from your final list will more than likely find their way into your envision sentence.

Once you send me your sentence along with your best 10 elements, I will guide you in the next step.

Warmest regards,

Mr. A

New York City

Aiming...

Wednesday, January 16, 1946

Dear Mr. A:

The process you outlined worked amazingly well for me! Ideas flowed and kept flowing, as you predicted. My goodness, I never knew how many ideas were inside me!

As a side note, when I was on the General's staff in the Army after the fall of Berlin I did much typing. So much so, that by the time I returned home I was able to type faster than I could write.

For this latest activity on envisioning I decided to use my typewriter, since I could produce very orderly notes quite fast. And, I did. The only problem was that my creativity was stymied. It felt like my 'idea pipeline' was clogged. So I returned to hand writing, and the ideas seemed to flow effortlessly from my pen to my paper. Mr. A, have you ever experienced this kind of phenomenon?

Returning to your letter, the quote from Hamlet: "Brevity is the soul of wit.", triggered an old memory. On my first day at the Grain Processing Company before the war, they had me clean up an old desk from a back corner of the warehouse for my use. It was full of old documents and magazines that I was told to organize.

For some reason the April, 1918 issue of the technical milling letter *The Operative Miller* caught my eye. Maybe because it was older than me. In flipping through it I spotted this quote:

"How long does it take you to prepare one of your speeches?",
asked a friend of President Wilson not long ago. "That depends
on the length of the speech", answered the President.
"If it is a ten-minute speech it takes me all of two weeks
to prepare it; if it is a half-hour speech it takes me a
week; if I can talk as long as I want to, it requires no
preparation at all. I am ready now."

I was allowed to keep this issue, and still have it today. In doing your process, this quote makes much more sense. Even President Woodrow Wilson agrees that brevity takes considerable effort!

I must tell you that it was not easy to keep narrowing my lists down. Nevertheless, I meticulously followed your instructions resulting in the final list of my best 10 elements combined from my dreams list and envisioning list.

Per your instructions I ranked the elements from 1 to 10, and then crafted the top elements into my envision sentence, which I have enclosed. After all my thinking and writing, I am pleased with the envision sentence. It really packs a punch!

I am amazed at how much more it says in fewer words than my original vision statement, that I wrote for the business plan I began prior to your process. Even still, my envision sentence seems a little too long, so perhaps you may have some suggestions for me.

Yet Mr. A, there is so much left unsaid. Your list reduction process and word limits force choices, *some very hard choices*! I am wondering, did I make the right choices? For example, did I cut some idea that I will need, or include some element that will be unnecessary? How do I know if I truly included the best ideas?

By the way, I am calling the company: The Food Transport Co. It doesn't seem terribly creative, but it does describe the company well. What is your reaction to this name?

I can't wait to hear from you in regards to my envision work. And just so you know, I feel more clear than ever before about the direction I am headed and I feel ready to "fire".

So, am I done with the "aiming"? Or, is there more to do? I'll wait for your reply before I pull any triggers!

With an itchy trigger finger,

Max

Salina, Kansas

~ *Max's Top 10 & Envision Sentence* ~

Combined from Dreams and Envisioning Lists:

- *the company is relationally focused whether it is an employee, customer or vendor [3]*

- *constantly creating and innovating new methodologies in the food industry, particularly distribution and transportation [5]*

- *become the premier food transport company in the Midwest and U.S. transporting food from the field all the way to the kitchen table [2]*

- *achieve success and profits to benefit the hungriest [8]*

- *encourage balanced lifestyles for all with whom we come in contact: family - work - social - philanthropic - health - spiritual [6]*

- *devise formulation to benefit the hungriest based on miles driven or amount of food transported for the company [9]*

- *always provide the freshest and healthiest foods faster and more reliably than anyone else [7]*

- *alleviate some hunger and suffering in the world [4]*

- *don't squeeze every nickel out of a deal [10]*

- *assemble a great team that creates a midwest (company) community that reflects friendliness and enthusiasm while delivering great products efficiently and fast [1]*

Envision Sentence:

To establish The Food Transport Co. as a premier company whose team loves to deliver the freshest, healthiest food from the field to the kitchen table, faster and friendlier than anyone else.

Steady..., Every Word Counts!

Monday, January 21, 1946

Dear Max:

Excellent work! But, ease your finger off the trigger. There is a bit more to do before the "firing" begins.

Ah yes, President Wilson's quote, I had forgotten it. Brilliant Max! It is quite prescient to The Navigator process, as you perceive. For brevity does require effort, much like that ten minute speech.

I am quite impressed with your results. Your list reflect a great deal of thought, and your sentence reads like a seasoned company's Envision Sentence, not a company yet to be formed. It will serve you well, as you will soon discover. Furthermore, I am gratified to know how my process is helping you.

Before going to the next part of the process, I would like to address a most important question you raise: "How do I know if I truly included the best ideas at this stage of the process?"

The short answer is: "You can not know at this stage!" However, your question points to another secret to success inside this strategic process. *If every element contains part of you, how can those ideas be wrong ideas?*

My hunch is that your best 10 list points to strong enthusiasms within you and reflects those characteristics that are most true about you. For example, phrases like: "relationally focused, constantly creating and innovating, become a premier, alleviate some hunger and suffering, don't squeeze every nickel out of a deal" all seem to describe your passions and authenticity.

In the film industry they say that some scenes of a movie end up on the cutting room floor. In the same way that not every scene filmed makes it into the final movie, nor will every idea make it into your company.

A great movie has just the right the scenes to tell a compelling story, so a great company will have just the right ideas. For a film to achieve that story the producer will continue to edit the film, adding and deleting scenes until the story he has envisioned emerges.

You, Max, are the producer of the company you envision. Keep all those ideas that are currently on "the cutting room floor". Adding or deleting ideas as the company launches and grows is quite common, and it is even a part of The Next Level Navigator process. The secret in the early years is to continue processing your ideas for the company's envisioned state by choosing, combining, and refining them until only the ideas that precisely reflect your vision are included.

Max, you are uniquely made. If the company is tethered to your passions, your desires and authenticity will keep you enthusiastically engaging in your company over the years. And if you are highly engaged, so it will be for everyone around you. That, my friend, is a secret to long term sustainability!

Refinements

In regards to your envision sentence, I do have several possible refinements.

You describe your company delivering "from the field to the kitchen table". I love the picture you create, but *is it factually true?* Check your thinking on this, as it may be inaccurate unless you are planning to eventually deliver directly to the end user, that is the consumer. My understanding was that you would deliver to retailers in the marketplace.

You might also consider changing "a premier" to "the premier" company which would signal you are envisioning a company that will be the best in its industry.

The phrase "...team loves" is terrific. Few companies rely on love, and yet it is the most powerful force in the world. Might the word "friendlier" be redundant, or at least to some degree diminish the impact of the action verb, "love"?

These thoughts may seem minor now, but every word in this envision sentence will greatly impact you and your company's orientation towards its future. How do these remarks seem to you?

Guiding Principles, instead of Core Values

Now let us consider Guiding Principles, another foundational element of The Navigator. In truth, these will be the foundation upon which your company is built!

Max, all organizations have core values or beliefs that are of central importance to them. Some companies state them plainly, others just operate from them not realizing their approach to business is built upon them.

By establishing these values before your company begins will give you and any future team of people you assemble a huge advantage towards operating as a cohesive unit. How?

By plainly stating your Guiding Principles you will naturally assimilate a culture of like-minded people who will typically work together much more easily and productively. Over time these Guiding Principles may be modified and tuned, but the essence of them will remain as the foundational building blocks upon which your company is established.

A typical *core value* for a service company could be: "We treat our customers fair and square." Notice the phrasing: it is a statement of fact. The implied tone is we do this every time. But what happens if a customer disagrees, is the company then not fair? Or, does the company change its methodology in that one instance to appear fair?

In truth, I prefer to call core values: *Guiding Principles to which a company aspires.* This name shifts the attitude to focus a bit more on intention which allows for occasional, honest failures. I suspect that is what most companies believe is implied with Core Values. So, why not just say that the company may miss occasionally, since failure is inevitable within any human organization. As you know, I prefer authenticity to overstatement.

Thus, my core value example restated as a Guiding Principle could read: "We aspire to interact fair and square with all our customers." Perhaps, you can see the slight shift in tone that communicates the company strives to never disappoint, but it may on occasion.

For an established company, listing its Guiding Principles may be as simple as adapting its existing Core Values; or at the most observing the way the company conducts itself and creating a list from observed values in action.

Guiding Principles for a New Company

For a company that does not exist it is a little tricky, but doable. Since core beliefs ultimately emanate from the founding entrepreneur(s), another angle on this application is to ask yourself: "What are yours?" In other words, the Guiding Principles for the company will source from your principles, beliefs and values.

So Max, since it is not always easy to observe ourselves, I would like you to cull through all your work with me from the beginning: your original dream list, disappointments, your authentic characteristics, even your disruptions will all contain clues about your values. Then, review your most recent dream list for your business and all your brainstorming for your envision sentence. Even your journal notes around these topics could be helpful.

The question to keep in mind during your review of these lists is: *What are the underlying core beliefs and values to these ideas?*

Practically speaking, here is an example of how these values could emerge for you. In reviewing the first 3 points on your original dream list I would suggest a key value such as: 'bold industry innovator' or mixing in your open range cowboy dream: 'a trailblazer'. Does this give you an idea on how to proceed?

So as you review a list, jot down anything that occurs to you that may be a principle, belief or value. Do not be concerned with duplications or editing the list. Once completed, I suggest you wait a day, as your mind will continue ruminating over these lists, perhaps uncovering other key values to add.

Next, identify any similar items and rewrite the list combining them. Remember not to just copy items, restate them with greater clarity and precision. Each principle included on the resulting list should be unique. Identify and rank the top principles up to 10, and set aside the rest.

The final Guiding Principles should provide strong guidance as to how the company operates while being easy to remember. Rewrite, edit, cut and restate the top 10 until you emerge with the most fundamental 3 to 6 principles. The Guiding Principles should feel very true to you.

Whenever you are ready, please send me a copy of both your final Guiding Principles list and your longer list, too. I am most interested in seeing them!

All the best,

Mr. A

New York City

P.S. As to your company name, I am not the best to ask. At the very least, it is a good placeholder name for now. Once you have The Navigator clear and your direction set, you could revisit the name with some good marketing folks.

Guiding Principles

· Monday, January 25, 1946

Dear Mr. A:

I can't describe the clarity and strength I have received from your Guiding Principles activity. It was wonderful to review all my previous lists and glean from them how I intend to operate. In fact, I found myself able to analyze my lists more objectively, as if they were written by someone else!

Mr. A you are absolutely correct that I do have Guiding Principles, core values and beliefs from which I operate, whether I am aware of them or not. Your process really helped me to discern them, and the list I have enclosed feels quite solid to me. I can imagine how these principles could be refined once the company starts operating, but clearly these are THE foundation blocks upon which the The Food Transport Co. will be built!

As to the envision sentence, I have taken your comments to heart. I like your suggestion concerning "the premier" and can see how it implies the best. In fact, by thinking through the Guiding Principles I realized if we are the freshest, then it would stand to reason that we would have to be the fastest. So, I am dropping the word 'faster' and opting for the word 'freshest', even though we are a transportation company.

Does this make sense? Do you think people will understand what we are about, if they see this sentence?

As to the 'field to the kitchen table', I have really thought about your observation. For now, I am committed to that picture. I am not sure how we will do it, but then *it is a vision*. I did drop the word table, because I do not envision us preparing and serving the food which could be inferred from including the word 'table'.

Mr. A, I really appreciate you teaching me how each word needs to have real meaning and impact.

I have enclosed the updated envision sentence, my brainstorming list on developing the guiding principles, and my final list. I did write an 'in between' list, but there were so many scratch outs and overwrites, I did not think you would be able to read it or follow it. So, I did not include it.

Ready for the next step,

Max

Salina, Kansas

~ *Max's Guiding Principles (draft & final)* ~

Updated Envision Sentence:

To establish The Food Transport Co. as the premier company whose team loves delivering the freshest, healthiest food from the field to the kitchen.

Guiding Principles Long List:

- *entrepreneurial mindset - willing to take initiative, navigate risks, produce great returns*

- *alleviate hunger where we encounter it*

- *financially strong company through growth and profits*

- *passionate team: everyone has a passion for what we do*

- *team has similar goals and beliefs*

- *on the cutting edge of constant innovation*

- *small town, midwest neighborly feel - friendly, help a stranger, relaxed*

- *family is important - the work supports all the families (of the employees) and the families support (the employees), i.e. the work*

- *everyone knows their role in the company and how they impact the company's direction*

- *the direction of the company is clear to everyone in the company*

- *keep the company friendly and relaxed*

- *co-workers are also friends*

- *honest in all our dealings*

- *deliver top quality food*
- *a portion of profits are siphoned off to feed the hungriest*
- *always asking: 'how can we do it better?'*
- *delivering faster and fresher than competition*
- *be the best - the premier*
- *most reliable - easiest to do business with*
- *relationally focused - a people first company*
- *constantly innovating - a trailblazer*
- *alleviate some hunger of the hungriest*
- *don't nickel and dime vendors or customers*
- *our word is our bond - full of integrity*
- *efficient, fast, fresh*

Combined Guiding Principles FINAL List:

The FTC, Co. aspires to

- *Establishing a relationally focused team with a people come first attitude.*
- *Trailblazing entrepreneurially by continuously risking and innovating.*
- *Producing solid returns through growth.*
- *Alleviating some hunger of the hungriest in the world.*

Deepening the Foundation

Wednesday, January 23, 1946

Dear Max:

I am writing this letter in advance of receiving your Guiding Principles, because I wanted to respond to your earlier question in regards to *hand writing versus typing*. Knowing you, I imagine you can not wait to start the next step, so I have included it, as well.

To be honest Max, I have a staff that handles all my typing needs, and I dictate much of my business correspondence. However, I am not surprised by your discovery.

Have you ever woken up in the morning with a great idea, but by the afternoon you can not remember you even had an idea? When I reflect my ideas onto paper through the pen in my hand, oftentimes more ideas emerge, they become more real, and I remember them.

My greatest creativity flows through the pen in my hand, not from my mouth in dictation or conversation. I can see how typing could block the creative flow. Unlike a pen, it requires brain power to operate, which is distracting, no matter how rote it may become. After all a good typist focuses on accuracy, not what is written.

I would suggest you pursue your discovery and hand write all the aspects of The Navigator process. Once you have the final version hand written, then type it to share with others.

Thus far, your work has been excellent. So, I would like you to add a finishing touch summing up the foundational elements of your company before we delve into the Next Level process.

I call it the *Company Promise*. It plainly states a pledge from your company and employees to every customer you will ever have. Similar to core beliefs, all companies have some kind of promise they make to customers. Yet, it is so much more powerful to state it plainly for all to know. Especially, in this highly competitive world in which we live. A company needs to robustly differentiate itself from its competitors.

Similar to developing your Guiding Principles, review all your lists and any notes to identify all the potential strengths of your future company. For example, some possible strengths might include a strong customer base, identifiable brand, superb team, fast turnaround, etc.

Admittedly, you are imagining strengths, but imagination is a powerful force that can bring into existence that which did not exist. To assist you, consider your envision statement and your guiding principles and answer this question:

"What would the company's future strengths need to be as it moves towards this envision statement with these Guiding Principles?"

My hope is that this question will help you see more concretely what will be required to operate the company. Once you have a list of strengths, consider this question:

"What could your customers expect as result of encountering your team and your services?"

Quickly list your reactions to this question. Do not ponder it, rather just make a fast list of expectations, thereby capturing your instinctive response.

As you have done before, circle key words, combine similar items, ultimately narrowing down the expectations into a phrase describing the customer's experience in 7 words or less.

Voilà! This is your company's promise to its customers. However, keep testing it to determine if it captures the heart of The Food Transport Company's customer experience you envision for now.

All the best,

Mr. A

New York City

Reliably the Freshest!

January 29, 1946

Dear Mr. A:

I must be learning your ways, because this Company Promise came rather easily and quickly. *It is a great finishing touch!*

Writing out my aspirations for the strengths of the company actually deepened my focus on what I hope the company will attain. Then, as I imagined the customer expectations, I realized how I want to raise the current industry standard.

Today, significant loss and shrinkage of perishable foods during transportation is not only expected, but acceptable. So, I wrote what I believe customers desire, not expect. If, my company could begin to deliver toward these levels I believe we could be "The Premier", and we would have as much business as we could handle. In other words, we could leave our competitors in the dust!

I realize there are huge realities today that prevent companies from fulfilling these customer desires. So, that is why I am convinced there are huge opportunities to innovate in this industry, even though it may take many failures to get there.

It was so amazing as I followed your process. I felt like the Company Promise literally wrote itself. Even after considerable reflection and testing, it feels like in 3 words the entire endeavor is completely summed up:

Reliably the Freshest!

What do you think, Mr. A? I have enclosed my list of future strengths and customer expectations for your reaction.

Best regards,

Max

Salina, Kansas

~ *Max's Company Strengths, Customer Expectations, & Company Promise* ~

Company Future Strengths:

- *Passionate and caring employees who are on-board with the company's culture and guiding principles*
- *Top notch logistics with the most up to date methods to track shipping and deliver quickly to reduce spoilage*
- *Innovating ways to handle product to eliminate spillage and shortages of loads*
- *Constantly improving its systems and methodology*
- *Fair in all its dealings with employees, customers and vendors*
- *"No questions asked" return policy*
- *Growth oriented without diminishing its services or culture*

Customer Expectations:

- *The company is the best in its field: delivering every load fully intact (with little or no loss), on time or even early.*
- *Even though customers may pay a premium price, the experience with us and freshness of goods far exceed any price differential with the competition.*
- *A company that can be relied upon to meet or beat expectations.*
- *Consistent and excellent in everything the company offers.*

Company Promise to Customers:

"Reliably the freshest!"

From the Journal of Mr. A

HISTORICAL NOTE:

According to Mr. A's journals from late 1945 through early 1946, he spent considerable time anticipating Max's answers to the questions and applications he was presenting through The Next Level Navigator process.

Mr. A writes that he did this in order to fully immerse himself in Max's ideas, thereby gauging Max's answers to his own, as a method to better advise him. It seems he was quite disciplined in not giving Max his answers or telling him what to do. Thus, he was able to draw out of Max his truest, fullest and deepest thoughts and ideas.

Mr. A also describes that he was intentionally guiding Max in some basic marketing concepts. By focusing Max on customer expectations and any potential competition he was helping Max draft his company's initial tagline and brand promise, as it is known today. We know this because the phrases Max uses appear in some of the earliest marketing materials of The Food Transport Co. Mr. A was remarkably ahead of his time, as are most successful entrepreneurs.

Although Max's company would evolve over the years into a global food distribution company, it is amazing how formative the initial Next Level Navigator was in shaping the company into what it is today. The concepts contained in Max's first Navigator would continue to appear in future Navigators and other company documents for decades.

The Next Level

Monday, February 4, 1946

Dear Max:

Great work! I love your company's promise: *"Reliably the freshest!"* You have said much in a few words. Brilliant brevity, Max *'Shakespeare'* North, or should I call you Polonius!?!

Your guiding principles are superb, because they distill what is most important in you to direct the company. However, it appears to me there may be a gap, as no principle seems to address the transportation aspect of your transportation company. For instance, how would you want the company to deliver goods? Perhaps this could be a fifth principle, which would not be too many.

One last thought to help orient you, Max. The Guiding Principles list is an inward facing statement from which a company operates. The Company Promise is an outward facing statement that lets the world know the experience the company creates.

To date, your diligence to The Next Level Navigator process is serving you well. I am struck by the genuineness and aspiration contained in your company's strengths, and the candor contained in anticipating customer expectations. It all seems quite realistic.

You have gone much further with this assignment than I could have imagined. Once the company is launched, remain alert for what strengths do emerge and what customers actually do desire.

Now, I want you to shift your focus to:

The Next Level phase of The Navigator process.

You may recall from a previous letter that I explained how a company's Next Level lies over the horizon. In other words, a company's leadership can know what the Next Level is, but can not see the path to achieving it. In terms of time, a Next Level is typically 3 to 5 years away. Every Next Level a company reaches, moves it that much closer towards its Envision Sentence.

Once a Next Level is identified, the Next Strategic Step can be determined. Its path can be known and achieved in about 6 to 12 months. Typically, after accomplishing several Next Steps, a company will reach its Next Level.

Do you remember my "prehistoric drawing" illustrating the Next Step in relation to the Next Level and the vision?

Max, keep all the work you have done in mind, especially your envisioning sentence. All this will be quite helpful in pinpointing your company's Next Level, which for you will be your First Level!

To begin identifying the Next Level imagine it is 5 years from now; February, 1951. In your imagination walk through the company and describe what you see.

For example: What do you experience as you walk through? How is the team? What happens when customers encounter your company? How are products handled and delivered? Observe the company processes and workflows. What is the company's organization like? Simply allow your creative power to freely associate one image or idea to another.

Jot any and all descriptors down. Make notes of every aspect that comes into your mind. Remember not to evaluate any idea as they occur to you, simply write them all down.

Now imagine you are in your office or conference room reviewing these past 5 years. Maybe you are with your key leadership team or board of directors. As you look back since the company's launch, what has most pleased you about what has been accomplished? What is going well in the company? What needs to be improved? Remember, it is February, 1951.

As you write down your answers to these questions, allow any other characteristics about the company to bubble up from your imagination. Be spontaneous and quickly write every thing that comes to mind. Do not ponder or over-think what you are writing. Max, the idea is to fully imagine the company 5 years from now and capture whatever you see. Any evaluation of ideas will come later.

Once you feel satisfied that you have captured as much as you can; review, organize, and rewrite your descriptions and characteristics of the Next Level. Based on those descriptors answer these questions:

- What is the purpose, the intent, and the motive behind this Next Level?
- What would mark the achievement of this Next Level? Describe it like a finish line crossed in a race. Keep in mind there can be multiple markers, finish lines or metrics, although preferably, not financial.

After decades in business one of my observations is that companies rarely celebrate achievement. In the sports world victory celebrations are built into the culture. However, many businesses have no finish lines, no winning score, no end of season champions and thus, no celebrations. Even companies that set goals, typically change them as or before they are reached. The goal's achievement is often relegated to that of checking an item off a 'to do' list.

Inadvertently, companies breed a culture that never realizes success and subsequently has no sense of finishing or accomplishment. What kind of life results from no celebrations, no parades, no hoopla? Human beings are designed for so much more!

You, yourself, heard General George S. Patton say this when he addressed the 3rd Army:

"When you were kids, you all admired the champion marble shooter, the fastest runner, the big-league ball players and the toughest boxers. Americans love a winner and will not tolerate a loser. Americans play to win all the time. That's why Americans have never lost and will never lose a war. The very thought of losing is hateful to Americans."

Achieving a Next Level must be definitive and should be cause for great celebration and satisfaction among every employee. Thus, it is so important that every employee have some role in propelling their company to its Next Level.

So Max, establish markers that clearly delineate when the company has achieved its Next Level. A company must know victory, so the celebrations may begin!

Once a Next Level is achieved and the company has celebrated, restart this process to create a new Next Level Navigator, but I am getting way ahead of myself. So, let us return to this application.

After you have written all your descriptions, characteristics, and answered the above questions, then express the company's Next Level in a single sentence of 25 words or less.

As with the envisioning sentence, begin with a paragraph of words and begin honing it into a single sentence. Use the rewriting technique I have given you until each word conveys significant meaning and the sentence precisely describes the company's Next Level. Keep remembering: *"Brevity is the soul of wit."*

Max, allow me to offer you one other secret: Write from the deepest, truest part of you, which is deeper than your 'gut' or intuition. Basically, attempt to bypass the brain with all its critical thinking, and tap into your truest desires and highest aspirations.

Over the years I have discovered that *my mind will produce goals, but my entrepreneurial desires will produce Next Levels.*

And that my friend, is how I dream big, while remaining true to who I am. This is the answer to one of your earliest questions.* It is how I view the world with infinite possibilities and not finite ones.

I eagerly await your Next Level sentence!

> Affectionately,
>
> *Mr. A*
>
> New York City

P.S. Max, allow me to reiterate that in your final list of markers, limit yourself to only one financial marker. Even then, I believe that may be one too many. Why?

If you make your company's Next Level all about your passions aimed at your envision statement, your passions will be inflamed and your motivations great! Success will be yours, and will extend far beyond monetary compensation. If the marketplace learns of your products or services and likes them, the money will follow as a byproduct.

* **Note:** See the letter dated Thursday, August 21, 1941. Titled: *That's It?*

Becoming Clearer

Monday, February 11, 1946

Dear Mr. A:

It has now been 4 years since I shipped out to Officer Candidate School. In some ways, it feels like a lifetime ago, and in other ways it does not seem that long ago. I am so grateful in the ways that you have come alongside me, both before the war and since my return.

Once again, your last letter has given me so much guidance, especially the new technique you offered me. It has been quite the challenge to bypass my brain and write from my entrepreneurial desires. I hope I did write from my desires to some extent, at least for a beginner!

This latest phase was amazing. Just when I didn't think I'd have anything else to add, your guidance drew out of me more vision and detail. In fact, in researching the grain business and talking with the general manager at the grain silo I have expanded the geographic goal to include Missouri.

As you will read, it makes sense to focus on delivering grains to flour mills and breweries, and then back hauling their products. Since, Missouri has numerous breweries, and Kansas has few; I have included delivering in Missouri as part of the Next Level.

What is so amazing to me is how the Next Level and the company are becoming clearer and clearer. In fact, the company is beginning to feel very real to me, having spent this extra time developing The Navigator. I have enclosed my lists and my Next Level sentence.

Oh, and Mr. A I did come up with another guiding principle. You were right, there was a gap. It was so obvious that I had provided no guidance for transportation which is what the company is all about! I guess that since transportation is the core of the business, I just assumed it was understood through implication. So, the 5th guiding principle is:

"Neighborly delivery of the freshest, healthiest foods."

Mr. A, I look forward to hearing your reaction and doing the next part.

With deep gratitude,

Max

Salina, Kansas

~ *Max's Next Level Description, Characteristics, Purpose, Key Markers, and Sentence* ~

The Next Level Description:

As I tour the company it is amazing to think it has only been 5 years. We are operating in our own trucking facility and warehouse. It is quite a busy operation!

We began renovating the old, eyesore building on the edge of town for our company several years ago. We only use as much space as we need, but we keep doubling every year, soon we may need another building, and this one is huge.

Team and Culture:

The team has really come together. Logistics, trucking and marketing all sync together very well. They are constantly innovating and sharing ideas across departments. We have been able to hire people with experience in logistics and transportation, and it has made all the difference. Even though much of the experience has been with armored vehicles and other military transports, it does translate to our industry. In fact, we have a high percentage of veterans working for us across the company.

There is a camaraderie and esprit de corps throughout the company that balances a military precision of delivery with a neighborly, down to earth, midwest personality.

Operations:

Our system of haul and back haul enhances our efficiency so that we can deliver fresher than anyone else. By initially focusing on flour mills and breweries we have expanded throughout Kansas and Missouri and now are expanding into bordering states, plus the Texas panhandle.

We have learned to stay focused on our core products that begin with grains for human consumption, as opposed to grains for livestock, etc. This means that we have turned down business. We are beginning to expand into various kinds of produce and are experimenting with delivering directly to grocery stores. We are listening to customers as to where and how to expand.

Finances and Giving:

This is a capital intensive business, so we manage our debt to equity carefully and will not grow faster than our cash flow allows.

The sweetest part of our success is that a portion of our profits are used to feeding the hungriest in the world based on miles driven. In fact, we have even driven our own trucks filled with food to some of the most hungry in Mexico and Central America.

Characteristics of The Next Level:

- *Operating out of our own facility*
- *Team comprised with experience in logistics and transportation (former military)*
- *Defined food products to haul*
- *Expanding from grains to produce*
- *There is a haul and back haul component to every customer relationship*
- *Delivering throughout Kansas and Missouri from grain silos primarily to flour mills and breweries*
- *Expanding network of customers into neighboring states*
- *Develop credit facilities to fuel growth while maintaining reasonable debt to equity*

- *Positive cash flow and profits*

- *Feeding the hungriest with a portion of profits*

- *Publish miles driven / pounds hauled to feed the hungriest ratio so everyone (customers, vendors, employees) knows how and who benefits*

- *Identify the hungriest we can benefit*

Purpose, Motive, Intent:

The intent of this Next Level is to develop a strong, profitable growing grain transportation company as a way to gain a foothold in the food transportation industry while alleviating some hunger of the hungriest. Once established, then survey and determine the next direction to achieving our vision.

Key Markers of Having Reached The Next Level:

- *Have our own facility*

- *Experienced team*

- *Expanded throughout Kansas and Missouri*

- *Profitable and alleviating some hunger*

The Next Level Sentence:

Establishing a strong presence in the delivery of grains to flour mills and breweries throughout Kansas and Missouri while alleviating some hunger among the hungriest.

Success Barriers

Friday, February 15, 1946

Dear Max:

It does not seem that it has been only four years since you headed out to Officer Candidates School. So much has happened! I am remembering how you seized the day by volunteering, as a result of the attack on Pearl Harbor. Since then, you have fought in a World War on two continents serving your country so admirably. I deeply respect you, Max North!

Frankly, your letter embarrassed me, as I have been so engrossed in The Next Level Navigator with you that I have failed to inquire about your well-being or recall your four year anniversary. Not only do I thank you for reminding me of what is truly important, but allow me a moment of personal confession.

Periodically, I become too absorbed in my work and lose sight of those relationships which I value so dearly. This weakness of mine has caused great pain in my past to those I cherish. Although I have made atonement, I still struggle. So, I am sorry for not being more attentive to our relationship. Please forgive me.

Let my behavior be an example of what to avoid. Cherish every moment you can with those who are closest to you. Honestly, Max I have come to understand that *success in this world is fleeting, but the treasure of close relationships, well those could be eternal.*

So back to true priorities, how are you doing with all your emotions, wounds, and memories in the aftermath of the war? I do care, and truly want to know.

In reading all your Next Level writings, I simply marvel at your work. It is so complete. All I can say is "Bravo!" I have nothing more to suggest at this point. Furthermore Max, I love the *"Key Markers"* term you coined and intend to start using it myself!

As you begin this next phase of the Navigator I must warn you that it could be emotionally risky. To prepare, carefully review all your Next Level notes, descriptions, sentence, characteristics, purposes and key markers. As you consider every aspect of the company's Next Level, answer the following question by listing everything that comes to mind.

What are all the reasonable barriers that could prevent achieving your company's Next Level?

By barriers I mean hindrances, complications, disadvantages, problems, etc. Write about anything that could keep the company from achieving its Next Level as you described with your Next Level sentence, characteristics, purpose, and key markers. These are the Success Barriers that hold a company back.

A word of caution: human nature tends to gravitate more towards the negative than the positive. Most people find it easier to assume the worst, list the negatives, or see the potential doom. This phase of the process begins by focusing on the negative, but it moves quickly beyond the negatives, and so should you.

So, be alert that listing Success Barriers to launching your company and achieving its Next Level could discourage and deflate you. Do not let it. Instead, I urge you to move quickly in developing your list, but do not dwell on it too long or over-think it. Fight any discouragement or despair, a normal reaction by any entrepreneur.

Now, STOP reading this letter. Do NOT PROCEED to the last page until you have completed your barrier list. As soon as you complete your list, please read the last page of the letter.

Due to the nature of this step I did not want you waiting for my next letter of instruction, so I have included it. I am trusting that you will not peek!

~ This letter continues on the next page. ~

Overcoming Success Barriers

*~ Final page of the previous letter dated
Friday, February 15, 1946. ~*

Max, only after you have completed your list of Success Barriers
should you continue reading. Now consider this question:

*"What would be a strategy to overcome each one of these
barriers on your list?"*

Give yourself some time with this question to let your creativity
and problem solving come to bear on each barrier before you write
anything down.

When you are ready, follow these steps with each barrier listed:

- Choose any barrier off your list or combine similar barriers.
- Restate any barrier(s) that need further clarification.
- Then devise a strategy to overcome that barrier and write out
  that strategy.
- Repeat by choosing another barrier until you have a strategy
  for each one.

TIP: I suggest you start with a few uncomplicated barriers for
which you can easily devise strategies to overcome them. This will
build confidence and help you shift into a strategy developing
mindset to tackle the harder ones.

Once completed, please send me your original barrier list with
the rewritten barrier list and the corresponding strategies. Oh, and
Max, please tell me how this exercise was for you.

Your friend,

Mr. A

New York City

Hindered by Hindrances

Tuesday, February 19, 1946

Dear Mr. A:

Your recent letter took me by surprise. After all your encouragement to envision, imagine, and dream about the future of this business venture; the last thing I expected from you was to list all the barriers and hindrances that could keep me from achieving that vision. To tell you the truth, as I read your letter and began listing some barriers, I began to sense some hesitations and fears that seemed to be lingering just below the surface of my life.

And boy, did those fears uncork the more hindrances I wrote. It was more than discouraging, in fact *my negative thinking exploded* into thoughts like: "I am just kidding myself", "this will never work", "I need to go find a 'real' job", etc.

You were spot on in your exhortation to "Fight any discouragement or despair", and I would add depression. So, I stayed faithful to you Mr. A, free thinking as many barriers, hindrances, or problems that I could. I gave myself a set period of time and in great detail went through all my lists visioning the company. I recorded every barrier that came to mind. I kept an eye on the clock, so I would not become bogged down. Managing the time was very helpful.

However, towards the end something snapped and I shut down. I guess I am still more fragile than I realized from my war experiences. I really don't know what happened to me. To be honest, there were moments when I would just rest my head on the desk, and my hands would literally shake. It was as if I could hear the sounds of battle in my head, and my body began to shiver. In my mind, I was experiencing past battles and firefights, my friends being shot, and that moment when I narrowly escaped death. I

166

began to weep, the pain that resurfaced seemed more than I could bear.

I can't go on Mr. A.

I don't have what it takes to be an entrepreneur, to start a company, and make it work, at least not right now. I am probably better at just taking orders.

I feel overwhelmed by these barriers and do not see a way to overcome any of them. I have enclosed my list so you can see how hopeless this business venture is. I never even read the last page of your letter.

At this point, I think it would be better for me to take the management position at the Grain Processing Company *with the hope that maybe one day I can pursue my dream*, at least partially.

Mr. A, thanks for all your help and encouragement, your advice has meant the world to me. Let's stay in touch.

Affectionately yours,

Max
Salina, Kansas

~ *Max's Success Barriers* ~

Guide to My Markings:

　　＊ *is a barrier to Next Level*
　　　　- *is my thinking behind each barrier.*

My Success Barriers List:

　　＊ *I have no foreseeable way to fund the business.*

　　　- *I have no borrowing history or significant collateral on which to borrow any money. Plus, I have no proven long-term income source to pay off any debt. Nor, do I know of any outside investors.*

　　＊ *What company would risk their transportation needs with my inexperience, even if I was capitalized?*

　　　- *I have no experience running an entire distribution company. I do have experience managing the shipping department of the Grain Processing Company (GPC) and assisted a little on the financial side of the business.*

　　＊ *Currently, I am alone in this vision.*

　　　- *I have no allies or partners with whom I can bounce any ideas off of and share future workload.*

　　　- *Plus, I have no sources for finding experienced people to help build the enterprise or a way to pay them.*

　　＊ *A distribution company needs trucks and fork lifts -- I have neither.*

　　　- *Furthermore I have no expertise with this kind of equipment: what it takes to operate, what is the right kind of equipment, how to maintain it, etc.*

　　＊ *The old, abandoned warehouse I had my eye on has been*

tied up in litigation over a disputed estate for years, now has city and county tax liens against the property for more than what it is worth. The county wants to condemn it and tear it down.

   - I am guessing it would take a small fortune to renovate it, and would probably be better to start with a new building, but may not be any cheaper.

* *Currently, GPC's transportation department is losing a lot of money. What makes me think I can do any better?*

   - I have no experience in turning around an unprofitable business, much less operating a profitable one.

   - I am an agriculture major, not a business major.

* *I only have one customer prospect, GPC. No marketing experience, no other prospects or industry contacts to even find prospects.*

The Telephone Call

Saturday, February 23, 1946

Dear Mr. A:

I was so surprised last night when I answered the telephone and heard your voice. I marvel at your touch; your wisdom; your grace; your timing.

I had barely said 'hello', when you burst into a soliloquy about how hope is not a strategy. I had no idea what you were talking about until you quoted the last paragraph of my recent letter: "...with the hope that maybe one day I can pursue my dream, at least partially."

Somehow you segued into your own version of having used hope as a strategy years ago to which I could completely relate. The way you told your self-deprecating stories about using hopes as strategies had me laughing so hard, tears were rolling down my face! Nonetheless, it was so illuminating when you revealed that your hope strategies were in reality only wishful thinking that led you to hopelessness.

As you told me about your breakthrough moment I was expecting a profound revelation, but instead you flatly concluded that all your hoping, i.e. wishful thinking, was a big pile of horse manure! The way you delivered that wisdom was hilarious!

Then you paused and explained, *"True hope is courage. Hope is allowing our deepest desires to burgeon into expectations that goodness is approaching."*

When you said that, I realized true hope summed up the Mr. A I know. Your soul is anchored in hope. You truly believe goodness is on the way. So it was hard for me to believe, that you of all people had had similar discouraging thoughts multiple times over the years, even to the point of quitting and failure.

However, as you began to call out my potential and what you saw in me, I was overwhelmed. The man you were describing, me, is not at all how I see myself.

I will never forget what you said: "Max, you have what it takes to be a splendid entrepreneur! I am sure your father would be very proud of you."

However, you not only deeply encouraged me, but you pointed me towards self-introspection and healing with a simply complex question: *"Max, what is all your despair really about?"*

I soon found myself telling you about war experiences that I had never told anyone else: details of my pain and loss and fear, oh and the anger and confusion. I spoke out loud stories I had never even heard myself describe, stories that went much further back than the last 4 years of the war, back into my days as a youth.

And the tears, well suffice it to say that there were piles of tissues on the floor by the end of the conversation. I don't cry, but somehow you get to me, Mr. A. Like at the dinner we had 4 years ago in Kansas City. You sneak up on me and the next thing I know the 'water works' are flowing.

I am realizing that something deep was touched in me last night in a cathartic way. It is hard to describe. Perhaps it is like multiple, non-physical injuries to my psyche of which I was unaware.

You guided me in forgiveness and release. Something I will endeavor to continue to practice. You pronounced healing over me. This morning, I am a different man. I feel an indescribable kind of peace about me or a relief, like a huge burden is being removed. My countenance is brighter. I feel more free and alive, than maybe I ever have. I think my entrepreneurial spirit may be returning, too!

Yet, even in the midst of me dealing with some tough stuff you acted indignant, in fact, hurt; that I would act as my own sage dismissing you so easily at the end of my letter! In an instant, you had me chuckling, even while the tears were still flowing.

Mr. A, you exposed me to myself in a way that was safe and kind. For in truth, I had lost heart and somehow you began to magically restore it. I marvel at your ease to move from thoughtfulness to playfulness, all the while staying on track towards my restoration. I deeply thank you!

And, I must say: *you are one helluva a sage!*

After your call I went back and reread the end of my letter. (I keep carbon copies of what I send you.) You were right! I was trying to be my own sage without even realizing it. Ok, ok, I yield. You are the sage! Not me! In fact, I commit to you that I will not try to 'self-sage' myself anymore!

As our conversation ended you encouraged me to continue with The Navigator. You explained: "of course these barriers seem insurmountable; otherwise, they would not be barriers...".

Then you revealed a most amazing secret: "*Great barriers lead to great strategies.* You have done very well, Max, in discovering great barriers, now it is time for great strategies".

Mr. A, I want you to know that you have reenergized me, and now I am refocusing. Today, I am pursuing strategies for each barrier per your instructions:

"Max, ponder each barrier and devise a strategy on how to overcome it. Write out those strategies and then discard the barriers. We are after great strategies, not great barriers. You will soon understand how this all fits together."

Already, the ideas for strategies are beginning to flow. I'll will send them soon.

NOT the sage!

Max

Salina, Kansas

Tactics vs. Strategies

Sunday, February 24, 1946

My dear Max:

You are such a joy! I was not certain how you would react to my calling you last Friday, but I must say that I love your responsiveness. You are one of the most teachable men that I have ever met, a most admirable quality, especially in a leader.

After our call, I began to reflect on my encouragement to you in writing strategies for your barriers. I believe I may have done you a bit of an injustice, for it seems that I have not provided any direction in how to write strategies. It is as if I have tossed you into a swimming pool supposing you can swim without any instruction.

Rather than assuming your skill level at devising strategies, permit me to provide some guidance by comparing tactics versus strategies. Many confuse these concepts and incorrectly use them interchangeably. However, they are distinctly different which is critical to understand, if you are to write effective strategies.

Over the years my experience suggests that most people are tactical by nature, meaning they do one thing after another without any overarching plan or sense of direction. Perhaps it is rooted in our basic need to survive.

For example, a person who is hungry needs money to buy food, so they locate a job. This instinctive reaction makes complete sense. A plan is devised and executed to solve the immediate problem at hand. This is clearly a tactic.

Tactics involve the specifics of how strategies are implemented.

Strategic thinking is less instinctive, and therefore rarer. In the previous example a strategy for the hungry person would be to seek a career that will provide long term support, removing hunger as an issue entirely.

173

Strategy involves the guidance to make decisions that achieve an overall outcome based on available resources.

Combining strategies with tactics is the best way to operate. The military illustrates this brilliantly, as I am certain you are well aware.

A classic example of a tactical maneuver in the military would be 'take that hill'. The platoon leader plans the assault and fights through to achieve the objective. But, to what end?

If it was only the platoon leader's idea, then it is a tactic with no over-arching strategic value and a waste. If he was ordered to take the hill as a part of an advance of multiple divisions, then it is clearly a tactic that supports a larger strategy to win the war.

Thus, strategies contain the concepts to reach the overall aim based on the resources at hand connected to the chosen methods to be used. The utilization of those resources and steps to take are found in tactics, i.e. carefully planned actions to achieve a specific end.

Typically, multiple tactics are required to complete a single strategy. Max, I believe you will find that most wars are won or lost at the strategic level, not the tactical level.

Let me hasten to add, this is not about controlling events to a desired outcome. Life simply does not permit that. In fact, controlling by its very nature eschews both strategies and tactics. Strategies, and tactics to some extent, create the opportunity for the opposite of control: *Freedom!*

All this leads us to a curious question: *If using strategy to direct tactics is so effective, then what keeps people from doing just that?*

One reason is that people can become pinned down by urgent issues. For example, when one urgent issue has been solved, it is quickly replaced by more issues, squeezing out any possibility of pausing to think strategically. I have found this to be particularly true in the world of business.

Another reason is the distinction between strategy and tactics are blurred. Both involve planning, implementing and flexibility to adapt to changing circumstances, all of which require good judgement. Thus, people may believe their tactical actions are actually strategic.

Max a great way to test if you have written a strategy or a tactic, is to remember:

A successful strategy shapes the future; a successful tactic achieves an immediate objective.

So the strategic question before you is "how would you like to shape your future?" Otherwise, you are left with this alternative question, "would you prefer to be shaped by the future?" Sadly, I find many resigned to this second question, leaving them to live from tactic to tactic.

Your first barrier beautifully illustrates my point: *"I have no foreseeable way to fund the business."*

If you allow the future to shape you, the response will be, "It will take years to build enough credit rating to even consider funding a new business. So, I will put my dreams on hold, and pursue the process of building good credit."

If you desire to shape your future, you acknowledge your reality of no funding ability and you begin to devise strategies to fund your endeavor and tactics to accomplish it

Great strategic thinking is circumspect. A word derived from the Latin: circumspicere, meaning 'to look around'. Look for all the possibilities in overcoming an obstacle, then formulate your best strategy. For example, one possible strategy for not having the requisite credit rating would be to find a partner who does.

Or per Brunelleschi's egg, an even more disruptive idea would be that you do not even need credit. To that end another strategy would be to leverage your talents off the needs of others in a partnering type of way. Or, create a strategy that utilizes customers deposits and vendor financing as a source of funding. Perhaps these strategy ideas will serve as an inspiration and example.

So my friend, now concoct strategies that will shape your future and overcome each obstacle. Think creatively like Brunelleschi! Do not accept status quo.

Will your strategies work? You will only know if you pursue them. Strategies do not guarantee success, but they do press against conventional thinking creating forward momentum. I have found that it is in the momentum where the opportunity for success lies. In other words, the strategy with which you begin may not be the strategy you use to achieve your ultimate end.

Meanwhile, consider the alternative: *Not* pursuing your dream. Well... at least not until you have credit worthiness much later in life when the opportunity will have passed and your enthusiasms for it are greatly diminished.

So, as you consider each barrier and concoct strategies ask yourself this question: *"Does my idea to overcome the barrier shape the future or does it merely achieve some immediate objective?"* In this way you will devise strategies that direct tactics.

I hope my letter enables you to 'swim back to the edge of the pool'. I look forward to reading your concoction of strategies!

All the best,

Mr. A

New York City

P.S. On a personal note, whenever I am creating both strategies and tactics, please know that I do so *"with a firm reliance on... Divine Providence..."*, similar to the Founding Fathers of this great nation. It can be so very helpful!

Concoction!

Monday, March 4, 1946

Dear Mr. A:

You will be pleased to know that I am back on track in pursuit of my entrepreneurial endeavor! Ultimately, I do want to shape my future, not be shaped by it. All the credit to my re-engaging belongs to you, Mr. A!

The turning point was during our phone call when you asked me "what is all your despair really about?" Your call broke my cycle of countless 'why' questions. It reminded me that prosecutors ask accusing questions beginning with 'why', rather than inquisitive ones using 'what'. My self cross-examination had been brutal.

Moreover, I had completely forgotten your question to me last summer when I was still in France: *"What path now?"* You showed me how that question can bring significant redirection coming out of disruption. You added that 'why' questions "will never lead you to creative choices." You are so right, Mr. A! I must train myself to ask 'what', instead of 'why'.

Also, I shared your despair question with two trusted friends. They know me and my story quite well, and provided me some keen, yet tender observations. Somehow, through them with your counsel, and that question; I am gaining deeper insights into myself.

One insight is that writing all those barriers somehow uncorked old and even deeper disappointments. And this triggered recalling and reliving the pains related to these disappointments.

Those memories occurred long before the war, much earlier in my life and go beyond our conversation several years ago at the hotel. All of that flooded me with confusing emotions from my past touching off battlefield flashbacks, so I simply shut down.

Now, I am beginning to see how those old hurts misshaped me

growing up. I have compensated for them through drivenness, excessive risk taking (like on the battlefield), and over reaction to other people's perceptions about me, to name a few.

Ironically, rather than feeling devastated by these revelations; I am sensing peace, relief, and even healing. In fact, I think I am beginning to experience some of the freedom you have described by living a little more into the person I am intended to be.

My worst fears that seemed so insurmountable have begun to shrink, and my creativity and energy are returning. Mr. A, thank you for all your counsel, encouragement, and prayers which have been so significant. It is nothing short of miraculous how quickly I have been able to restart my strategy development. I am quite excited to continue refining them.

Your question: *"Does my idea to overcome the barrier shape the future or does it merely achieve some immediate objective?"* is a wonderful way to test my ideas to overcome each barrier.

By applying your test I can see that I had written many tactics, including financial ones. It even revealed some were not even tactics, really just measurements of a tactic's success.

Your strategy test has guided me in writing much better strategies that capture the *'who'*, *'what'*, *'where'*, *'when'*, *'why'* of what I need to do. Frankly I'm amazed at my 'concocted' strategies!

Even though I am feeling great about them, I realize that even now there may still be some lingering tactical thinking. So, please shoot straight with me and expose any tactics you spot.

I've enclosed the barriers with my corresponding strategies. What's next, my invaluable mentor and friend!?!

Sincerely,

Max

Salina, Kansas

~ *Max's Barriers with Overcoming Strategies* ~

<u>*Guide to My Markings:*</u>

* *Success Barrier to Next Level*
  - *Strategy to overcome barrier*
    • *Sub-strategy*

<u>*Success Barriers with My Strategy to Overcome:*</u>

* *I have no foreseeable way to fund the business.*

  - *Already, the Grain Processing Company [GPC] favors me and would like to rehire me into their upper management. My sense is that they believe I would add value to their company in a high profile position. So, apply that value to help launch this endeavor.*

  - *Seek a partnering relationship with GPC by offering a plan to assume responsibility for their transportation department. Begin operating the company inside GPC leveraging off their desire to hire me, but instead hire my company for the same cost.*

  - *Use the goodwill from my military experience and solid reputation as a leader to begin establishing relationships with investors and bankers in the area.*

  - *Start operating the company with 'sweat equity', meanwhile begin establishing any kind of credit to prove trustworthiness and ability to repay debts.*

  - *Live off my army back pay and not draw a salary. I can probably do this for at least 2 more years.*

  - *Avoid outside investors, preserve the company's equity for company leaders / managers.*

✳ *What company would risk their transportation needs with my inexperience, even if I was capitalized? I have no experience running an entire distribution company.*

   - *I do have great experience and success in leading men. So, apply my leadership to this business venture by finding men who have experience in this industry and lead them.*

   - *Since, the transportation department of GPC is not their core business and they would rather not do it, especially since it is losing money, counter the GPC job offer with a proposal that I partner with them as an independent company to run their transportation department by taking over its operations for the same cost as what they'd have paid me in salary and benefits.*

     • *We would continue operations in their facility which would reduce their risk with us. They would be able to observe how we are doing. Establish some oversight guidelines they would retain while we are on site.*

     • *Define a transition period of a few years, during which time they would continue to pay their current level of transportation expenses while I transform the transportation operation.*

     • *At the end of the transition period the transportation department would be owned by my company for the depreciated value of the assets we are using and would be moved to its own location.*

     • *My company and GPC would split any expense savings (after my additional cost) during the transition period, thereby potentially increasing their profitability during the transition period.*

     • *GPC would still gain the value they perceive in*

having me as part of their organization. Plus, additional goodwill down the road as they help me become an independent company. (a win - win)

- *By operating the transportation department as a stand alone company within GPC, we would grow in experience, plus have access to their experienced leadership team for guidance.*

✱ *Alone in this vision. I have no allies or partners; no sources to find experienced people or ability to pay them.*

- *I did know some excellent Non-Commissioned Officers and Officers in the Transportation and Quartermaster Corps that helped support our armored vehicles, etc. Track them down. Find those who could manage logistics, transportation, and maintenance. For key leaders, offer them equity in the company as long as they remain and in exchange for some 'sweat equity'. I have several men in mind, as possibilities.*

   • *Develop a pool of contacts from which to hire.*

   • *To participate as owners, they would need to live at a least a couple of years on their back pay and not need to draw a salary, the same as me.*

✱ *No sources for finding experienced people to help build the enterprise or a way to pay them.*

- *We will take on those GPC employees that currently help run the transportation department that seem to be a good fit for our future company.*

- *Network with former military personnel through the future core team's contacts that were in the quartermaster or transportation corps.*

- *Over time build our company's culture and team.*

* *Do not have any trucks and fork lifts. I have no expertise with this kind of equipment: what it takes to operate, what is the right kind of equipment, etc.*

  - *Propose to GPC that we take over the equipment we think we need and operate it during the transition for the cost of maintaining it while we are on their premises. When we move, we will have the option to buy the equipment for a predetermined amount based on the depreciated value that GPC would be willing to help finance, since they will no longer need the equipment.*

* *The old, abandoned warehouse has been tied up in litigation for years and now has city and county tax liens against the property for more than what it is worth.*

  - *Negotiate with the 2 parties for the estate to abandon the property to the city/county in exchange for all back taxes, fines, etc. being zeroed out. Negotiate with the city/county to establish a 100 year lease with us for a next to nothing lease rate provided we clean up the exterior, so it is not an eyesore. Their incentive is that this would bring another viable business with jobs to the county. It would be a win-win-win for all parties.*

  - *Begin renovations at our expense. If needed the county could be a guarantor on a loan to expedite renovations.*

  - *Since these negotiations and renovations will take a while, this will give our new company time to become established and ready to move to its own location.*

* *Currently, GPC's transportation department is losing a lot of money. What makes me think I can do any better?*

  - *Put together 'turn around' strategies by talking to several businessmen I know who faced similar situations for their companies in the early '30's. Hear both success and failure stories from which to develop strategies.*

    • *Focus exclusively on grain transportation and be the best at it.*

    • *Tour other operations (in other states that are not competitors) and see how they do it.*

    • *Streamline both the transportation and maintenance departments' processes, roles, responsibilities, etc.*

    • *Cut expenses. Negotiate with GPC to use only those assets, resources, employees deemed necessary.*

- *Add additional customers to broaden the revenue stream and cover expenses.*

- *Develop a 'back haul' business, so that both legs of a trip create revenue which GPC is currently not doing.*

* *I only have one customer prospect, GPC. No marketing experience, no other prospects or industry contacts to even find prospects.*

- *Develop relationships with prospects and vendors, instead of selling / marketing. I am not a salesman, but the way I lead men is by developing a relationship with them using persuasion (not orders) as a way to get things accomplished.*

    • *Utilize my reputation as a way to connect.*

    • *By operating the GPC transportation department, I could begin with all the customers / vendors of GPC.*

    • *Between GPC and my reputation the new company will have strong credibility. By having a transition period it will provide time to develop relationships and expand our customer base.*

    • *Thus, we will have a track record of success.*

Beyond Rewriting

Monday, March 11, 1946

Dear Max:

Considering that you were walking away from your entrepreneurial vision when we spoke by phone 17 days ago, to my receiving your strategies in today's morning mail, clearly I am witnessing a deep breakthrough in you. I must confess that I am astounded by the rapidity of your rebound!

In all honesty, you have taken my little question: "what is that despair all about?", much further than I ever dreamed. Your insights on the differences between 'what' and 'why' are brilliant, and precisely the basis for my question.

Furthermore, I applaud you for being vulnerable with your two friends. Having close allies of the same gender in your life is of an inestimable value, whether you are a man or a woman. Oh there is so much more I could say on this, but I will save it for another time. For now, keep those two men close!

Essentially what I am hearing from you, is that you have battled through more than barriers to write a few strategies. Rather, you are overcoming hindrances within yourself that would eventually keep you from achieving all you are intended to be.

Max *a little known secret* is that in most cases for a breakthrough to come about in an entrepreneurial enterprise, *the breakthrough must first occur in the entrepreneur leader(s)*.

And so it is with you! The initial fruits of your breakthrough are your strategies, which are fantastic. There is much creativity, insight and energy contained in them. Truly you are on the verge of completing a most excellent Next Level Navigator.

Yet, something even greater than a Navigator may be emerging. I believe the true Max North could becoming visible, maybe for the first time. Considering all the disappointments, hardships, and disruptions throughout your life; it seems that this process is bringing you freedom from those things. Max, I can see grace at work in you, and you are responding. You have persevered to the finish!

In fact, what if the ultimate objective of your engaging in this entrepreneurial endeavor is for you to fully live into the life for which you were intended?

Remember my telling you that "great barriers lead to great strategies"? Well, a corollary to that principle is:

The person who overcomes will find great fulfillment, clear identity, an overflowing life, and more!

Max, you are overcoming and moving towards the role only you can play. You are ready to lead this venture! And, the venture is almost ready to be led. But first, there is one more phase that involves refining the strategies, which will be much more than rewriting.

The strategies you devised are currently written and organized in relation to each barrier. Now, you must revise each strategy apart from any obstacle. So, discard the barriers for they have served their purpose of drawing out of you these strategies.

A practical way to both eliminate the barriers and improve the strategies would be:

- Cut your paper into strips so that each strategy is separate and throw away the barriers.
- Then group similar strategies together.
- As you consider each strategy ask yourself if it can be accomplished within 12 months or if it will take longer, thereby creating 2 groups of strategies.
- Now, recast, rephrase, and reword the strategies in your 2 groups. Be creative and recognize that other strategies may

occur to you, so include them.

- Order the groups of strategies in the sequence you would want to accomplish them.

- Now rewrite your strategies. Recognize that in regrouping them some strategies could be merged or changed.

- Finally, test and refine each strategy to ensure that it advances the company towards its Next Level. Keep in mind that this process may require several drafts.

- Review the 12 month group in the order that you would do them. If possible, estimate the time to accomplish each one. By creating an initial order with an estimated timeline your venture will become more tangible and measurable.

Please, send me the updated strategies when you are done. I will review them as any potential partner or investor or banker might, and reply with any questions or comments.

In the meantime, I will send you The Next Level Navigator format that you will use to organize all your work onto one page. This format can serve as your summary presentation of your business venture to others and also be used as a guiding internal document to launch your company.

All the best,

Mr. A

New York City

The Next Level Navigator Story

Wednesday, March 13, 1946

Dear Max:

It occurred to me after posting my last letter that you might enjoy the story behind The Next Level Navigator. Realizing you are in the midst of completing your strategies, please allow this letter to serve as the 'behind the scenes' of The Navigator, so no response is needed.

Also, I have enclosed a blank Navigator form for your reference. Once I receive your strategies, I will guide you in completing it.

So, how did The Next Level Navigator originate?

~ Invisible Barriers ~

Max, it all began when I was several years into my first entrepreneurial venture many years ago. The company was growing quickly and staff was being added to keep pace with the demand for our services and products. So, a person or two were hired at a time. The struggles began when the company reached about 25 employees.

As I recall, it was estimated that the company needed about 35 employees. However, as the staff expanded to 26, 27 or even 28 persons; a couple of employees would depart and the total staff count would fall back to around 25. This turnover pattern continued for almost a year which was undermining the business' growth and impeding its success.

It felt as if we were hitting some kind of invisible barrier. Nothing like this had ever occurred in the history of the company. After all, it was now the ripe old age of four! As the turnover continued we interviewed those leaving, reviewed our processes, had open conversations with the current staff, but no substantive answers resulted for us to act upon.

~Exhausted and Feeling Like a Failure ~

Meanwhile, I was working more and more, 60 to 80 hours a week, trying to keep up with everything going on in the company. Our sales were great due to our excellent marketing, but production was lagging and complaints were mounting. Towards the end of our fourth year, I was exhausted and ready to quit. So, I decided my best exit was to sell the company.

One prospective buyer made a very low offer which he kindly explained to me. His honest assessment was personally devastating. He described my company as "breaking at the seams to grow", observing that I was not able to manage all the key elements of the business. He surmised that I may have even been losing touch with some parts of the business. It was his opinion that significant investments in the company would be required to increase its value to justify my asking price.

Max, I felt like a failure. I politely refused his offer and decided to do what I had *not* done in 4 years: take a few days off. The truth is that I had only taken off one afternoon for a dental appointment and one day for jury duty in the past 4 years.

~ Escaping to the Hills ~

I felt like I was in a dense fog. Do you remember the valley I described in an earlier letter? Not only was I in that valley, but I was surrounded by fog. I felt trapped, so I headed out of town to a remote property in the hills for a few days alone. I had no plan, no agenda, and no ideas.

I did some hiking and fishing, but mostly canoeing. And oh, how I remember those naps in the hammock with the cool breezes rocking me! I had no idea just how exhausted I had become; how I desperately needed to clear my head and unwind. Oddly, I was shocked at how hard it was to do nothing! It seemed impossible to simply be alone in the quiet.

On my last day in the late afternoon I built a fire by the lake to enjoy the early evening and sunset before heading home. Sitting by that fire, poking at it, and enjoying the last rays of the sun setting; it slowly dawned on me. Could the invisible barrier keeping the company from success be me? For over a year, maybe 2 years, I had not been able to keep abreast and manage all the elements of the company. Twenty-five employees was as big as the company could grow with me working virtually around the clock! In fact, if I was to work less to have a life, the business would need to shrink.

Max I learned 2 important things in that moment: first, decompressing from a hard driving pace is hard, but when you do all kinds of creativity and insight can be unleashed. Second, I realized that it was I who needed to make a fundamental change to my approach, if the company was to break this invisible barrier (which I would later call a Success Barrier).

~ Willing to Transform to a Next Level? ~

In other words, we had gone as far as I could; and now some kind of transformative process was needed if the company was to reach its Next Level. It would have to be radical, and the company and I could not be the same after it.

But, how? Would I be truly willing?

As quick as I thought the phrase Next Level, I recognized that it precisely described what had occurred since the launch of the business. In only 3 years the venture had reached a new level and plateaued.

As the fire popped and crackled, it became painfully obvious that I had not been adapting, so by the fourth year the company had stopped growing, turnover soared, and customer complaints increased. My solution? Work longer and harder, which was killing me and not changing the negative trajectory of the company.

As I stared into the fire, a sad reality about me began to become clear. My soul was dying or maybe it was already dead, and I did not even know it. I had no life outside of work, few friends, forgotten interests, and zero other activities. I was a completely secular, work absorbed man who had become incredibly shallow and two-dimensional. My work life had become the sum total of my life, and it was failing. Max, *I had become quite the boring fellow*!

Now a few twinkling stars began to appear, as embers from the fire rose to meet them. Watching them dance in the growing darkness, I was thinking through all the aspects of my company. I knew the company really needed over 50 employees. Yet, I was stretched far beyond my capacity with 25. I can still remember that night. My mind was whirling.

~ A Change of Plans ~

What was I to do? So, I did the most preposterous thing (for me): I broke with my plans and decided to stay at least another night! And, I am so glad that I did.

The next morning while drinking my coffee at the old table on the porch, I began to list all the things about the company that had to change. Soon it became obvious that list was taking too long. So, I listed the company's current strengths that were absolutely essential to our breaking through to a new level. That list was much shorter! Interestingly, these strengths were similar but so much deeper than those original ones when I launched 4 years ago.

I paused for lunch and a little canoeing on the lake. I kept asking myself, "But, where are we headed? What is that Next Level for the company?" Keeping up with customer demand and doubling sales were some of my initial thoughts. But, how was that a new level?

We could do that right now, if we increased the staff. That is when I realized that *a true Next Level can be described, but the path to it can not be known.*

I headed back to my spot on the porch and began by writing 150 employees as the Next Level. Even as I wrote the number, I knew that would be more of an indicator we had reached it, than the description itself. However, I needed something huge to spark my mind to describe a true Next Level beyond seeing the path to accomplish it. For there was no way I could envisage how to reach a company of 75 employees, much less 150.

It worked. I began to write and write. I wrote descriptions and markers and characteristics. I remember trying to summarize all of those pages into one paragraph. It was crude, but a picture of the company's Next Level was emerging.

Max, it may please you to know that I had all kinds of lists. Lists of what was good about the company that we needed to keep doing (our current strengths) and what we needed to stop doing. I listed ideas of where we could be headed (our Next Level) and how to measure it.

Staring at all these lists a new question emerged: "How?". What was the next step? Or, even better, what would be the first step?

~ Despairing, Again ~

By now, it was mid-afternoon, the hottest part of the day. My earlier enthusiasms were diminishing, and as I reviewed the Next Level a thought, more like a whisper, occurred to me: "this will never happen". It felt so true. To this day, I am not sure if it was the heat, my tiredness or that I skipped a nap; but I began to list all the reasons my Next Level description could not be achieved.

The reasons mounted, actually they were significant barriers to overcome. One barrier led to another. And Max, I quickly found myself utterly discouraged and ready to quit again. Does this sound familiar? Somehow, I had returned to the same state I was in when I departed town. I left my papers and collapsed in the hammock, very sad. Tears began to trickle down my cheeks.

I had no idea how long I had been sleeping when I suddenly awoke, it was early evening. I decided to pack and go home. I was done, and the company was done. I would shut it down, lay everyone off, which would be really tough, and go find a 'real job'. Surely, someone would hire me. Looking back, I now see how fragile I was in that moment. I was past hurting, I was numb.

Heading towards the cabin, I spotted the fire pit by the lake and could sense how pleasant it would be to have one more fire and enjoy the sunset before facing the inevitable ugliness of the coming days.

~ One Last Campfire ~

As the campfire flickered to life, I instantly knew this was good for my weary soul. I will never forget that fire. It was the best one I had built during the trip (maybe the best ever in my life!). I grilled the remaining fish on the open fire reviving me and immensely satisfying my hunger. But what occurred next made this fire unforgettable.

I became strangely still.

For the first time in 4 years or more, I was quiet, quiet on the inside. My mind stopped all its spinning of thoughts; I had no thoughts, just awareness. There was no restlessness, no anxiety or any pressure. It seemed as if a peace descended upon me, and I relaxed. Well not exactly relaxed, rather I rested, but not like in the hammock. This was different. It was outside of me, but surrounded me, and inside me, too. I knew complete relief and comfort. A gentle freedom washed over me.

~ The Disruptive Answer ~

Then, I heard what I can only describe as a still, quiet voice within me say: *"You are my leader, so lead."* This was completely different from the whisper of fear and doom I had heard in the afternoon. I can only surmise the voice was that of Providence. For with those words came an immense sense of calm and love, frankly it was indescribable. In my gut I knew these words contained my destiny. Every cell in my body knew these words were truth, exposing the earlier whisper as false.

This interruption of my dinner was *a disruption by relief!* And so, very unexpected. Now, I knew I was no longer dining alone. The sunset was at its peak, the fire was burning nicely, and the fish were indescribably delicious.

Yet those disruptive words continue to reverberate inside me, and I found myself exposed. For, I had always seen myself as a doer, someone who accomplished things. Now, I realized that I held a kind of disdain for leaders, who I perceived were not nearly as productive as I was. *Yet, my company was failing due to lack of leadership, not lack of doing!*

That was when I came face to face with the key barrier keeping my company from reaching its Next Level: *me.* I was, in fact, the barrier. It was in that moment Max, that I received and accepted *my new identity and role,* "You are my leader, so lead."

I knew I had much to learn about leadership and what it takes to become a great leader, but something immediately shifted in me as I accepted, what I would later refer to as, my new calling. Instantly, I began to visualize the strategy to overcome that barrier of employee turnover. For that was the one barrier above all the others with which I had been mentally wrestling all afternoon, even while asleep!

~ My First Strategy ~

I could see myself leading a team, even while being on the team. I envisioned other team members fully empowered to lead the areas of operations, sales, services and product. In the blink of an eye, I knew who to tap for each role, while I would continue in the marketing and financial roles. My first step to our Next Level was the strategy to establish a leadership team and empower them.

I was elated! I had a breakthrough! I had a strategy to overcome one of the most challenging barriers. It seemed the fog was becoming a little less dense, and a fresh hope began to bubble up inside me. Instead of laying off 25 people, we could eventually provide employment for 125 more! I rushed back to the cabin and found my barriers list. I returned to the fire, chose another barrier, and created another strategy. I knocked out quite a few that night by the light of the fire.

(As a side-note: Later after my return, various employees would confirm that I indeed was a barrier to growth by all my doing and not trusting others with important tasks. Some people left the company frustrated by me. Apparently, some even resented me.)

By the next morning, my whole demeanor had changed. The company's Next Level was not only possible, but probable. I was ready to return home, but only after a huge breakfast. I can not ever recall being that hungry. My appetite was restored, which was a very good sign.

~ Returning to Pursue The Next Level ~

Upon my return to the company, I immediately assembled the new leadership team. I took them through all my notes and the methodology that had emerged during my time away. I was stunned by their contributions and enthusiasm. It was like strapping jet engines on to a prop plane. I could not keep pace, and it has been that way ever since. They improved all my ideas, took ownership of their areas, and we began to move forward to our Next Level.

Max, this did not mean it was all smooth sailing. Oh there were numerous rough spots, but we did achieve our Next Level in about 3 years, long before our 5 year target. It may interest you to know that one of the Next Level markers was that my work week would average less than 50 hours and I would take whole weeks off for vacation. It took a few years, but slowly I began to rediscover how to truly live a full life.

~ The Next Level Navigator Works! ~

To mark the achievement of our Next Level, we had a huge company-wide celebration which included 128 new faces among us! Equally important, the leadership team collaborated on our second Next Level Navigator. This time all of us went out to the hills together. We found that we had new and expanded strengths, bigger barriers that required more powerful strategies to achieve an even more ambitious Next Level.

After a few years we formalized the process that creates The Next Level Navigator. Today, The Navigator is such a significant part of our culture that it has established a strategic rhythm within every corner of the company. We involve every employee in its achievement, so that everyone owns a piece of the Next Level.

This is the very same process through which I have been guiding you. I hope you find this tool to be as helpful in launching your venture, as it has been for me.

All the best,

Mr. A

New York City

Enclosure: The Next Level Navigator form

begin
__/__/____

Next Level Navigator for _____

complete
__/__/____

focused
released
empowered

Next level sentence: (3 to 5 years)

Purpose:

Key Markers:

Characteristics:
- A
- B
- C
- D
- E

↑

--- Success Barriers to break through ---

Next Strategic Steps: (in 1 year)

1. a
2. b
3. c
4. d
5. e
6. f
7. g

Strengths to build on:

Envision Sentence:

Guiding Principles:
- a
- b
- c
- d
- e

Company promise:

Strengths:
- A
- B
- C
- D

Culture:

An existing company's needs to transform building on its strengths

An Easy Conversation

Tuesday, March 19, 1946

Dear Mr. A:

It is wonderful that my energy and enthusiasm has been restored, as there is so much going on and even more to tell you.

But before anything else, I must share my response to your Next Level Navigator story. Since it arrived, I have read it and reread it.

My first reaction? You really did understand my struggles with barriers, even to my shutting down! After several readings, I am perceiving there are mysteries about you that seem to deepen, even as you reveal more about yourself.

Suffice it to say Mr. A, I am utterly transfixed by your story behind The Navigator. First, it brings so much understanding to this strategic process. But, what has truly captivated me is the transformation that you personally experienced. Clearly, you reveal an encounter with the Divine. I am most intrigued and desire to know more.

Once again, you were so correct, that this next step was "much more than rewriting". In fact, the more I have reworked all the strategies, the more energy and enthusiasm and belief I am finding for them. This is the exact opposite of what I expected. In fact, my enthusiasm bubbled over in an amazing, happenstance conversation!

Yesterday, I encountered the owner of the Grain Processing Company (GPC). We fell into an easy, albeit brief conversation. Before I realized it, I began sharing a bit about my ideas, really my strategies, on solving their transportation issues. He was immediately intrigued and told me that he would very much like to hear more, whenever I was ready. He confirmed that they were losing money in their transportation area and added that it was becoming a huge distraction from their core business. I surmise that he needs to take action soon.

Mr. A, I can't begin describe how much hope this gives me. All my strategies hinge on this one idea: begin operating my company inside GPC. I am stunned. These strategies could actually work! This business venture could actually launch!

I have enclosed my rewritten and reorganized strategies for your reaction. It is still a work in progress. I have lost count of the drafts. Even though the strategies seem wordy to me, I want you to review them. Frankly, to refine them much more will be tough.

The strategies are organized in the approximate order they would be started. However, I have not included any time frames, as I am perplexed how to do so. Some strategies must be accomplished simultaneously, others are dependent on the results of particular strategies, which those results would determine other strategies to pursue or not pursue, etc. I am hoping you will understand.

Although this list of strategies does not reflect it, I have an idea of which ones could or need to be accomplished in the first 12 months.

With all that in mind, I would most appreciate any suggestions on how to finish. And Mr. A, at this moment I am so full of gratitude for you and your friendship with me! You are truly an extraordinary man who has greatly impacted me!

With deep gratitude,

Max

Salina, Kansas

~ *Max's Detail List of Strategies* ~

1. Propose to the Grain Processing Company *(GPC): Rather than me working as a full time employee, instead hire my company to operate their transportation department as an onsite partner for the same total cost of hiring me.*

2. Complete negotiations with GPC that include:

    2.1. Define a transition period of 18 - 36 months that ends with our moving to our own offsite facility.

    2.2. GPC would continue to cash flow the transportation expenses at the current level during the transition period.

    2.3. After my total cost is added in, any expense savings (from the current expense level) during the transition period for the delivery of the GPC grain would be split by the 2 companies, thereby potentially increasing GPC's profitability during the transition period.

    2.4. Any outside revenue generated by my company would belong to it less any additional / pro-rata expenses.

    2.5. My company would have complete control over which employees work for the transportation company and what equipment we utilize.

    2.6. We have complete freedom to hire and operate within the cash flow of the company / current expense level.

    2.7. We can not fire any current GPC employees that transfer to our company, rather we will transfer them back to GPC. Every employee will have a say in which company they work for.

2.8. Establish guidelines between the 2 companies so that GPC has some oversight of operations but cannot direct it. The idea is to keep GPC fully informed, able to provide feedback, and that all grain transportation will continue as well or better than before.

2.9. I would publicly appear with GPC so they could still benefit from the value of my association with them.

2.10. Predetermine the purchase price of any assets my company may choose to purchase that is currently being utilized by the transportation department. The price would be based on the depreciated value of the asset at the time of transition. The assets will be financed by GPC at predetermined rates and terms.

3. Establish the new company from day 1 while keeping the transportation department operations the same.

4. Begin establishing relationships with local bankers and investors based on the goodwill from my military experience and proven leadership reputation. Cultivate their interests in my business venture for possible future financing needs.

5. Reduce my personal expenses as much as possible and live off my army back pay to launch this endeavor. Plan to do this for at least 24 months.

6. Organize the company with 2 other key leaders in the following roles.

6.1. I will lead the overall company business development, strategy and growth with at least a 51% stake in the company.

6.2. Second key leader will be over all operations and

directly lead transportation and maintenance.

6.3. Third key leader will be over all administrative functions and directly lead all logistics.

7. *Search for the 2 key leaders by contacting several former top-level NCO's and Officers I worked with in the Transportation and Quartermaster corps to partner with me in this endeavor.*

    7.1. To qualify for any ownership they must be willing to forgo at least 24 months of salary and live off any army back pay or savings they may have.

8. *Network with former officers and NCO's in the Transportation and Quartermaster Corps for any good men they know for us to consider adding to our team.*

    8.1. Whereas on the outside we want our customers to experience "neighborly delivery" behind the scenes I want there to be a military precision to our execution and ruthless pursuit of innovating improvement.

    8.2. Whereas there are some fine people working at GPC they may lack a preciseness that I believe is a source of some of their losses.

    8.3. To succeed I think this culture has to change.

9. *Once we are in charge of the transportation department, develop a transition plan and turnaround strategies for it beginning with the personnel.*

    9.1. Gather input from businessmen I know who have faced similar situations of losses before profits or lost their business altogether. Utilize their experience and wisdom to put together turnaround strategies.

    9.2. Network with other transportation operations of

non-competitors to share ideas and tour their facilities.

9.3. *Evaluate employees over the first 90 days and begin implementing the transition plan.*

10. *Generate positive cash flow within the 1st 6 - 12 months and create profits within 12 - 18 months.*

10.1. *Evaluate and begin cutting expenses.*

10.2. *Look for ways to increase efficiency and streamline processes*

10.3. *Expand customers to increase revenue include hauling and backhauling opportunities.*

11. *Market the company through developing relationships with prospective customers.*

11.1. *Get to know people in the industry and for them to meet us. Establish our reputation through relationships and performance.*

11.2. *Begin with whom we are delivering grain for backhaul opportunities.*

11.3. *Identify and begin talking with other grain processors as potential customers.*

12. *Based on the promise of revitalizing an abandoned, eyesore property and bringing more jobs and commerce to the area: Negotiate with the 2 parties of the estate and the city/county to cut through years of litigation in exchange for all back taxes and fines being zeroed out. The county would take over the property, and establish a 100 year lease with us for a $1.00 a year. We will clean up the exterior and begin renovations at our expense. To expedite renovations the county will act as a guarantor on a loan of our choosing. This could be a win-win-win for all parties.*

Completing Your Navigator

Monday, March 25, 1946

Dear Max:

My sincerest congratulations on your well done conversation with the owner of the Grain Processing Company!

The fact that it was unplanned for you to speak extemporaneously made it a watershed moment, when you could either soar or fail. To be honest, I would have suggested you avoid such a high risk moment. However, that sentiment probably reflects a softening of my entrepreneurism; whereas, I imagine your contagious passions came through boldly.

Max, the owner's positive response to your ideas indicates you soared. Men of his caliber are not easily persuaded to such unconventional ideas.

All your hard work in thinking through the elements of The Next Level Navigator have prepared you in a way in which you may be unaware. Without rehearsing, you knew exactly what to say, because *you are internalizing your Navigator.*

Furthermore, you were forced to be succinct due to the happenstance nature of the encounter and deliver the essence of your entrepreneurial idea quickly with just the right points.

Rambling thoughts are easy, undisciplined, and rarely impact. Your short conversation reflected you grasping that *'brevity is the soul of wit'*. And that my friend, is why you have been invited to present your full plan. So, you must move with all haste! Moments like these must be seized, or lost forever.

~ Finished! ~

Max, having reviewed your strategies and learning of this conversation, I can confirm that you are finished with the process and ready to complete The Next Level Navigator one page format!

Allow me to add that it is incredibly helpful to hear from someone outside of ourselves when we are done, especially in regards to strategic planning. I find people either tend to not think their strategies through enough or they over-think them. The secret is to do just enough. As that outside person to you, I declare that *you have done just enough.*

Using the blank sketch of The Next Level Navigator format, I will guide you in completing your final version! The beauty and frustration of this one-page is its limited space. Max, you have sent me many pages of thoughts and strategies, and I know that you have written much more than what I have seen.

So, now is the moment of truth: how can you say all that in one page? Actually, you already have. What did you say in your happenstance conversation? *Those words and that audience is your best editor!*

~ The Final Step ~

The starting point is the bottom section of The Navigator. It establishes the company's foundational strengths and identity upon which the Next Level will be built. This is what is best and lasting about the company! Typically it includes: the envision sentence, guiding principles, company promise, culture characteristics, plus any other unique or differentiating strengths of the company. For an ongoing company, this section reflects what will remain once a company reaches its Next Level.

Once you have established the company's starting point, the next question is: "Where is the company headed?" The top section of The Navigator illustrates the company's Next Level. Remember Max, the clearer one's Next Level, the more likely it will be reached. The Navigator needs two dates. The date you will begin the

Navigator, and the date you anticipate reaching your Next Level. You may recall that a Next Level is typically reached in 3 to 5 years.

Begin the section with the Next Level sentence. A real secret to success is for every person in the company to be able to express it with understanding. It is also critical to establish the finish line, to know when the Next Level is reached. These are the markers. And finally, to help everyone imagine the company at its Next Level list the top descriptive characteristics.

A company can know its Next Level, but not know how it will get there. So what are the first actions the company must take to begin to achieve its Next Level?

The middle section contains those Next Strategic Steps. These are the overarching strategies the company believes will break through Success Barriers to achieve its Next Level. This section is more fluid, since these steps are usually accomplished in 6 to 12 months.

Max, in this section you might consider having two sets of strategies: Next Strategic Steps strategies and future strategies, those strategies you foresee will follow The Next Steps when accomplished. I have found it helpful to place future strategies here, so they are not forgotten.

Finally, there is the breakthrough arrow on the right. In the circle, write several words that summarize the company's strengths or current condition. Above the tip of the arrow summarize the company after it achieves its Next Level in 3 or 4 words.

Once done, you have completed your first Next Level Navigator! Congratulations, Max!

~ The Power of The Navigator ~

Max, the secret to successfully launching your venture is constantly referring to your Navigator! This may sound obvious, but you would be shocked to discover how many people file away all their planning or lose it in some desk drawer.

Instead, I encourage you and your future team to use this document to launch and operate your new business. Show it to the owner of GPC and any other potential investors or lenders. I have found it to be an excellent recruiting tool, as well. People will be impressed at how quickly they understand your business and where it is headed.

Furthermore, consult it often. We dedicate one of our monthly leadership meetings to review and check the progress of all our strategies in relation to our Next Level direction.

The more you use it, the more you internalize it. The more you internalize, the more real it becomes. The more real it becomes, the more likely you are to achieve it!

~ Updates ~

Typically, we refine The Next Strategic Steps about every six months after it has begun. As strategies are accomplished the company's path to the Next Level becomes clearer, and these strategies will be replaced with new strategies. However, the Next Level markers remain basically the same, and as they are accomplished we note the date beside them.

Once they are all done, we have a grand celebration. Thus, every 3 to 5 years we completely start afresh with a new Next Level Navigator using this process. We begin with a blank page and establish a whole new Next Level.

Max, I hope this is clear and I look forward to reading your first Next Level Navigator!

All the best,

Mr. A

New York City

NOTES: New Companies Making Navigator Pivots...

Mr. A describes in his "Essence of The Next Level Navigator": *"Typically, new companies will make several significant pivots towards their Next Level, often requiring updates to their first Navigator."*

We have found in other notes of Mr. A's that he actually recommends that companies just starting out seriously rethink their Navigator each year of their first few years as a new business. Or, when the company realizes they need to make a pivot off their original direction.

He notes that it is not unusual for the entrepreneur and leadership team to require several years to settle into their truest direction including both the Envisioning and Next Level. Essentially, it is not until one fully immerses themselves in the marketplace do they actually begin to fully understand the dynamics of the market forces in relation to their Envisioning and Next Level.

Thus Navigator Pivots are normative for companies in the early years.

The companies that follow this advice often experience a beneficial side effect: they embed strategic thinking into their company's culture. Mr. A found that true strategic thinking is rare in most companies, so this provides a distinct advantage to new companies trying to compete.

Max's Next Level Navigator

Tuesday, April 2, 1946

Dear Mr. A:

I have enclosed my Next Level Navigator! I am amazed at how clearly it summarizes all my thoughts. You are the first person I have shown it to, and I can't wait to know your reaction.

At first, it seemed daunting to reduce all my work to one page, but using my audience as a filter unquestionably helped me choose what to include. You were right again, Mr. A! Not only did I consider the owner of the Grain Processing Company *my audience, but I included myself, too.* Blending the two perspectives honestly helped me know what to include and what to set aside.

By the time I started going through all the strategies, it was not that hard to boil them down to 7 summary strategic steps. Due to space, I did not include any future strategies, but I do have them listed in a separate document.

I must tell you Mr. A, that your process of taking lots of ideas and strategies and rewriting them over and over for clarity and brevity really works. It has truly helped me know my Navigator, or as you say, "internalize it". I find that it is very easy for me to expand on any point in it without notes.

As I step back and look at The Next Level Navigator for The Food Transport Co., it is absolutely stunning to me how real the company seems after completing your process. I believe this Next (First) Level is totally achievable!

I would still like to write a business plan to outline the details not included in The Navigator for key leaders/partners, GPC, and bankers or investors. But, I know it will be considerably easier than the one I started before your process. In fact most of the plan is contained in my Navigator notes.

Already, I have started the financial projections and they are so much easier to do with The Navigator in hand, as opposed to a few months ago when I was struggling and had no idea where I was headed.

As I await your response, I will also be drafting the key points for an agreement with the Grain Processing Company.

One last question, Mr. A: If you had never met me and I was showing you my Navigator for the first time, how would you react?

With immense gratitude,

Max

Salina, Kansas

Enclosure: My completed Next Level Navigator!

Next Level Navigator for The Food Transport Co.
Established
with strong,
delivery
presence

Next level sentence: Establishing a strong presence in the delivery of grains to flour mills and breweries throughout Kansas and Missouri while alleviating some hunger among the hungriest.

Purpose: To develop a strong, profitable growing grain transportation company as a way to gain a foothold in the food transportation industry

Key Markers: Have our own facility ~ Experienced team ~ Expanded throughout Kansas and Missouri ~ Profitable and alleviating some hunger

Characteristics:
- Team comprised with experience in logistics and transportation
- Operating out of our own facility
- Hauling and back-hauling throughout Kansas and Missouri between grain silos and primarily flour mills and breweries
- Positive cash flow and profits and feeding some of the hungriest
- Expanding from grains to produce

Success Barriers to break through

Next Strategic Steps: (in 1 year)

1. Complete negotiations with the GPC, launch FTC, operate the transportation dept.
2. Search and recruit for the 2 key leaders with whom to partner who were top-level NCO's in the Transportation and Quartermaster corps.
3. Develop and implement a transition plan with turnaround strategies.
4. Network with former officers / NCO's in the Transportation and Quartermaster Corps to find any good men they may know for us to consider adding to our team.
5. Market the company through developing relationships with prospective customers, key business leaders, bankers and investors.
6. Generate positive cash flow <1st 12 months and turn profitable <1st 18 months
7. Begin negotiations for the abandoned warehouse on the north side of town.

Strengths to build on:

Envision Sentence: To establish the FTC as the premier company whose team loves to deliver the freshest, healthiest food from the field to the kitchen.

Guiding Principles:
- neighborly delivery of the freshest, healthiest foods
- relationally focused team through a people come first attitude
- entrepreneurial leadership to continuously innovate
- produce solid returns through growth
- alleviate some hunger of the hungriest

Untested,
inexperienced,
but strategic,
relational and
passionate

Company promise: "Reliably the freshest!"

Strengths:
- Passionate and caring employees
- Have top notch logistics for tracking shipping and delivery
- Innovating ways to handle product
- Fair in all its dealings with employees, customers and vendors

Culture: There is a camaraderie and esprit de corps throughout the company that balances a military precision of delivery with a neighborly, down to earth, midwest personality.

Well Done!

Sunday, April 7, 1946

Dear Max:

Well done! I am so pleased with you! Your Next Level Navigator is fantastic, one of the best I have seen.

Your diligence, your hard work, your persistence, and your creativity to complete The Next Level Navigator have all paid off handsomely. You are a most remarkable man. All this preparation will serve you well. Your leadership comes through in every part of The Navigator.

To answer your question directly, if I were reading this for the first time and had just met you; I would be mightily impressed. Your plan is superb! Rarely do I see such clarity in thinking, which my experience suggests increases the odds of success, thus I would be an investor.

Of course there are no guarantees in life, as our best plans may not work. But having been on the battlefield you already know that. So, if and when things go awry you will know how to best respond based on your Navigator, because you clearly know where you are headed and how to navigate barriers with strategies.

Your Next Level Navigator is your best guide in "putting foundation under…" your "castles in the air"! And that my friend is *how you build a great company*!

I do have only one tiny suggestion to your plan, since you have yet to begin: change Next Strategic Steps to First Strategic Steps.

Other than that, I would meet with the owner of the Grain Processing Company as soon as possible.

So proud of you,

Mr. A

New York City

We Have a Deal!

Easter Sunday, April 21, 1946

Dear Mr. A:

Happy Easter! Normally, I do not work on Sunday, but I simply had to write. I am breathless, no stunned, actually elated, even relieved; really I am all of that and more!

Mr. A, it was unbelievable. I met with the owner of the Grain Processing Company yesterday for a one hour meeting at 9 am in the morning. Yet, the meeting kept going. Every hour he kept telling his secretary to cancel his next appointment, and then he canceled his lunch meeting. We finished about 2:30 in the afternoon.

Oh my Mr. A, I am absolutely be jiggered by his response. We started with The Navigator. He was completely intrigued and impressed. In less than hour, he wanted to know every detail. Fortunately, as an afterthought I had grabbed all my folders of notes and had them in my briefcase.

I wish you could have seen it. We moved into his conference room, and I had papers spread everywhere: details of strategies, Next Level characteristics, more guiding principles, even my dreams. It looked like my briefcase had exploded.

He had lunch brought in along with a huge chalkboard, and he was filling up a notepad with his notes. Soon, we were outlining our deal on the chalkboard. Our deal!?!

Mr. A, did I say I was be jiggered by his response? He totally believes in me and my approach and wants to partner with me and my (soon to be established) company. He wants me to finalize my business plan and he will write up the deal we worked out.

By the way he is willing to fund the transition because at the very least he is getting all of this for the same cost of hiring me, and at

212

best he reduces his cost overruns which could produce profits. This is everything I had hoped for and so much more.

He wants to begin the transition no later than 30 days from now, sooner if possible. Fortunately, I had already sent letters to three men that I would love to have work with me in this venture. Two, sound really interested, and they would be perfect.

Mr. A, it was The Next Level Navigator that opened this door. No, *it flung this door wide open!* Thank you, thank you, thank you! I owe all this to you.

How astounding that it is Easter Sunday! A day that celebrates new life and freedom. I feel like I have been resurrected and given a new life. A year ago I was part of the advance to battle for Berlin in which we had experienced some of the most brutal death and destruction of the war. Today, it is as if my life has been returned to me! And Mr. A, you have played a huge role in my restoration.

I owe more than this opportunity to you, I owe you my life! You ministered to me in New York upon my return, and you have counseled me through the colossal disruption of my life. Mr. A, you have poured so much into me, you believed in me and through you I am finding healing, peace, and freedom.

Yes, freedom! Just like that quote by your office door from the Declaration of Independence: *freedom to pursue my dreams,* those things that are the most true about me.

Oh, I know there is great risk ahead and potential loss and even more suffering. But ahhh..., the fresh air of freedom Mr. A, as you know there is nothing like it.

And now, I am breathing it in. Do you see what I see?

The potential to *form a great company* that could begin feeding the hungriest. Those that are hungry are very real people, just like you and me. They have no clue when or from where their next meal will come. I saw them in North Africa, even some in France and Germany as we were liberating them. And, I know they live everywhere, even in Kansas!

Oh Mr. A, thank you for speaking into my life and helping me find this freedom. I am more energized, more alive, than I have ever been!

Thank you, so very much. Mr. A, I am really out of words to express my gratitude.

With deep affection,

Max
Salina, Kansas

Epilogue

"The man who has lost the spirit of youth is too busy with gloomy forecasts...

Men with the spirit of youth pioneered our America...

Men with vision and sturdy confidence. They found contentment in the thrill of action, knowing that

success was never final and failure never fatal.
It was courage that counted.

Isn't opportunity in America today greater than it was in the days of our grateful forefathers?"

Live Life... Every golden minute of it

~ excerpted from a 1938 Anheuser-Busch Ad

Dear reader, this last letter is for you:

Max is now trekking into new and unexplored territory! He is leaving behind the path of his life that he knows so well.

He is on the cusp of beginning to *build a great company*. In truth, Max can't believe that he is about to launch The Food Transport Company! But, it is no accident.

He has invested time in *focusing his passions*. Additionally, he has discovered more about living into his true self and what he brings to his new endeavor.

Moreover, he has *mapped his direction* by developing The Next Level Navigator into a fine plan.

As Mr. A observed: *"The truest things about you are your best guide to your best future."* And, that is precisely where Max is headed. This is evident to anyone who reads his Navigator. Just as it was to the owner of the Grain Processing Company.

Yet, there is another ingredient that must be included. Remember what Mr. A once wrote? *"The best assurance of success is the intense look in the eye of the entrepreneur and the fire in his belly to succeed, no matter what."* And Max has both!

Now Max is about to enter the arena of entrepreneurism. He is embarking on the dream he listed first in his dream list: *"to pursue my vision, not someone else's"*.

So how about you? What are your dreams? What arena would you love to enter? What is stirring in you? What are some of your entrepreneurial desires?

Do the *Sage Advice to Apply* to find out. Follow Max's lead and create your own Next Level Navigator. You may be very surprised,

As you focus your passions, map your direction,
to build a great company!

Or, pursue greatness in whatever arena you choose for your Navigator. Regardless, you will begin discovering a freedom you have never known, like Max.

What's that? "It won't work for me", you may be thinking.

Do not listen to the negative voices in your head or the naysayers around you, instead dream big! (Reread pages 12 and 13.)

What happens after Mr. A's last letter? Max does start The Food Transport Company. And apparently, he needs Mr. A more than ever!

I say apparently, because more letters and journals and notes have recently come to light between these two men.

Now that Max has joined Mr. A in the same arena, their friendship deepens even further. In fact, there is a page 2 to The Next Level Navigator that Mr. A introduces to Max.

But, that my friend is another tale that I hope to share with you soon.

~ The End ~

More Resources to Reach Your Next Level!

As Max writes to Mr. A:

*"...I would prefer to chart my own course,
rather than work as a part of another person's vision."*

To that end, we've launched:

Live Truly Free

www.LiveTrulyFree.com

To help every entrepreneur at any level
"chart their own course"
by providing practical business guidance and strategy.

You're not alone in your **Entrepreneurial Trek.**
We're here to come alongside you!

So...

What are you needing as an entrepreneur?
Please tell us at

www.LiveTrulyFree.com/trek

And let's make

Live Truly Free

your 'go to' site for entrepreneurial help!

Plus...

**We would love to give you a FREE copy of
The Next Level Navigator form!**
(like the one on page 196.)
www.LiveTrulyFree.com/trek

A Closing Word from George

Now that you have read *The Next Level Entrepreneur*, I thought you might appreciate knowing a little something about me and my reasons for writing this book.

I love entrepreneurs! And I mean 'entrepreneur' in the broadest sense: *Any one who has an idea to make this world a better place.* I am especially excited for those who act on their idea.

My greatest passion in life is to encourage and assist every person I meet to *Live Truly Free*! Free to fully live into the person they are intended to be.

And the same goes for you, dear reader. Furthermore, I hope you achieve all your Next Levels, as well.

I would love to see a rippling effect that as you find new freedoms and Next Levels, you share these possibilities with others; whether in business or at a place of worship or charity, or in school, and especially with a spouse and your family and friends.

For me all this started when I began to leave the 'safe' paths in my life and became an entrepreneur, albeit my launch was somewhat atypical. This is how it all began.

Over 25 years ago, a friend of mine from a home church group would meet me for lunch every couple of months and ask me questions about his roofing and construction business. Each time we sat down he would say that he did everything that I suggested from our previous lunch and he was making more money than ever. I wondered what in the world had I suggested!?!

As he told me, my reaction was that I need to start doing those things, too! At the time I was managing parts of the operation and sales of my family's retail business that sold high end, residential furniture. However, my education and passions were in business finance and strategy.

Within a couple of years, I was on my own as an entrepreneur. I teamed up with entrepreneurial business owners to help them grow their businesses as their Outsourced Chief Financial Officer (CFO).

And, we did just that! Precisely like my friend, they were finding new freedoms by relieving financial stresses and having more time. About 10 years into 'CFO-ing' I was challenged with the question: "What is your process?"

My answer took several years of experimentation to ascertain, but it resulted in the strategic process I now call The Next Level Navigator. As I started using it with small companies, I found that it worked every time!

In 2004, I faced my biggest test. Could I organize all the ideas of the newly formed Enterprise Division of Rackspace Hosting into a coherent strategy? Using The Next Level Navigator, I did. It was such a success, that the CEO asked me to do the same for the entire company.

Over the next few years I helped guide both the corporate strategy and strategy of many of Rackspace's divisions with The Navigator until they went public in 2008 (NYSE: RAX). During that time the company grew worldwide from about 800 to over 2,000 employees, while revenues grew from $100m to $500m.

After such success, I knew The Navigator could help any individual, entrepreneur and company reach their Next Level. Concurrently, a deep desire began to form in me to share this process with everyone.

Hence, *The Next Level Entrepreneur* was conceived and written out of my passion and with Divine Inspiration. Now anyone can experience The Next Level Navigator for themselves!

By 2013 the 1st edition was published on Kindle. The next year Dr. Stephen Takach and I tested the book in his university senior level Strategic Management courses. His students did all the Sage Advice to Apply and Next Level Navigator exercises in the book.

The results were stunning! By following the book, each student clearly *focused their passions*, tied them to a business endeavor or their personal ambitions, and developed a Navigator to *map their direction*. We discovered 2 things:

First, the most repeated comment was that their business or personal idea was now very real to them and seemed very achievable. This continues to be one of the most common reactions to a completed Navigator.

Second, The Next Level Navigator works well for either a business or an individual.

Soon, many of the readers of the e-book began requesting a printed copy of the book, but the writer in me knew it could be much better. So, I deepened and expanded the content and published the book you now hold: *The Next Level Entrepreneur*.

What's next? *Live Truly Free* is our Next Level!

LiveTrulyFree.com is a site for every entrepreneur who wants to *"chart their own course"*. Please come and engage with us! We are adding more content and resources all the time to help you build a great company and find new freedoms as a person.

To inspire you on your Entrepreneurial Trek, we would love to give you a FREE Next Level Navigator form (see page 196). Simply go to www.LiveTrulyFree.com/trek.

Oh, and I should tell you that there are more letters from Mr. A and Max yet to publish, including a second page to The Navigator!

So, stay tuned and may you *Live Truly Free!*

George Black
San Antonio, Texas
April, 2019

About the Author

George Black guides entrepreneurs / business owners to develop their best strategies, create sustainable profits and build a great company.

He is both an entrepreneur and author.

Plus, George loves entrepreneurs!

He wants every entrepreneur to reap the same benefits as his 1 on 1 clients. So, George shares the same proven processes in *The Next Level Entrepreneur* that he has used to help numerous entrepreneurs, business owners, and companies for years.

Now, he and his team have launched *Live Truly Free* at LiveTrulyFree.com to begin providing even more resources for any entrepreneur who wants to build a great company.

Since 1992, George has worked as a Business Strategist and Outsourced Chief Financial Officer (CFO) through his company Intigro, www.intigro.com, where he created The Next Level Navigator®.

His clients have experienced significant growth, great breakthroughs, and increased profits.

Most notably, he applied his expertise and The Next Level Navigator at Rackspace Hosting for 4 years. He helped guide their corporate strategy as revenues grew five times to $500m and their going public (NYSE: RAX).

His client's have been located across the U.S. and internationally and in such industries as: technology, software as a service, manufacturing, commercial sales, professional firms, engineering, construction, government contracting, and not for profits.

George resides in San Antonio, Texas and has 2 sons. Some of his other passions include backpacking, travel, healthy living and helping 'the least of these'.

Made in the USA
Columbia, SC
21 June 2019